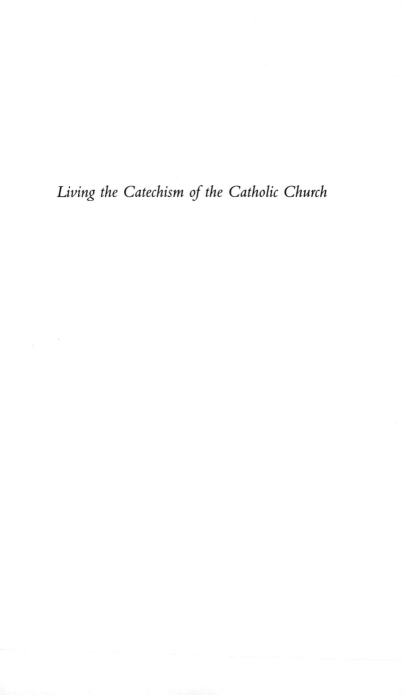

Living the Catechism of the Catholic Church

CHRISTOPH SCHÖNBORN, O.P.

Living the
Catechism of the Catholic Church

*A Brief Commentary on the Catechism
for Every Week of the Year*

VOLUME FOUR
PATHS OF PRAYER

TRANSLATED BY MICHAEL J. MILLER

IGNATIUS PRESS SAN FRANCISCO

Title of the German original:
*Wege des Betens: Das Gebet
in Katechismus der Katholischen Kirche*
© 2000 Dom-Verlag, Vienna

English translation of the *Catechism of the Catholic Church* for the
United States of America copyright © 1994, United States
Catholic Conference, Inc.—Libreria Editrice Vaticana.
English translation of the *Catechism of the Catholic Church:
Modifications from the Editio Typica*
copyright © 1997, United States Catholic Conference, Inc.—
Libreria Editrice Vaticana.

Cover design by Riz Boncan Marsella

© 2003 Ignatius Press, San Francisco
ISBN 0–89870–956–3
Library of Congress Control Number 95–75670
Printed in the United States of America ∞

Dedicated
in thanksgiving
to the many
quiet people of prayer
in our Archdiocese.

Contents

Foreword

The fourth part of the *Catechism of the Catholic Church* is the shortest. In many people's judgment, it is also the most beautiful. Again and again one hears the advice: Begin reading the *Catechism* here, with this part.

The original text was composed in Lebanon, in the midst of bombardment during a terrible war. Even though it underwent many revisions before the final version that was approved by the Pope, the strongly Oriental character of the draft is still clearly recognizable. The Holy Father had stated explicitly that he wanted the *Catechism* to "breathe with both lungs" and to unite the Western and Eastern tradition. What better place for that than with the subject of prayer, and especially in an exposition of the Lord's Prayer, the Our Father, which unites all Christians, all the baptized, in the shared grace of being children of God?

The fifty-two short chapters of this book (a one-year cycle of weekly columns for the Vienna archdiocesan newspaper) are by no means intended as a substitute for reading the *Catechism*. They should nevertheless be a stimulus, and they are also meant as an aid to reading it, but above all they are an invitation to the reader, encouraging him to turn to prayer himself. As important as guides to prayer are, nothing and no one can equal the "interior Master", who speaks to us in our hearts, who awakens the longing to meet him, who by his Word and his grace opens the eyes and ears of our hearts, so that we may come to know him, become well acquainted with him, and allow him to counsel and guide us. May the often awkward words of this little book serve the workings of the interior Master and thus allow him to speak for himself!

+ Christoph Cardinal Schönborn
Archbishop of Vienna

Feast of the Transfiguration of the Lord
August 6, 2000

While praying, we are never alone

What is more personal than prayer, "conversation with God"? And yet at the same time it pertains so much to all mankind; it is something that can be found in every age, in all peoples and cultures, as a personal or as a communal turning to God. One can describe "the world of prayer", and for this purpose there are large, thick volumes, for instance, *Das Gebet* [Prayer], by Friedrich Heiler, which devotes more than six hundred pages to depicting the prayer customs of various religions. One can elaborate the theology of prayer, the methods of prayer, and what the great Christian masters have said on the subject. All that is interesting; indeed, it can be helpful. The decisive thing, though, will always be the question, how do we learn to pray ourselves, and how do we live our life of prayer?

Du fragst mich, wie ich bete [You ask me how I pray] is the German title given to a book by the British Christian author C. S. Lewis [originally published as *Letters to Malcolm: Chiefly on Prayer*]. "Lord, teach us to pray" (Lk 11:1), ask the disciples of Jesus. The yearning for prayer can burst quite unexpectedly within our hearts, like a call, like a mating call: "Come!" This longing to enter personally into the world of prayer can also be kindled, though, when we see other people praying.

So it must have been for the disciples when they saw the Master praying, often into the late hours of the night, or even the whole night through, solitary and yet not alone, but rather completely outstretched toward the One who is invisibly present, whom Jesus calls "Abba, Father".

In prayer there are joys that cannot be compared with any other joy, and at the same time prayer is a constant struggle. But in either case we do not do it alone: we pray as members of a great praying community—and it is much larger than we can suspect—and we do not struggle alone to pray. Many invisible helpers—in heaven and here on earth—are with us and assist us.

Lord, teach us to pray!

There is a well-known incident from the life of Saint Edith Stein in which, even before her conversion, she goes into the cathedral in Frankfurt and sees a simple woman come in from the marketplace, kneel down, and pray.

According to Edith Stein's own testimony, the impression that this scene made upon her was a decisive moment along her path to faith: a simple person kneeling and praying in the cathedral. It is something inexpressible, quite simple, that you could almost take for granted, and yet so mysterious—this intimacy with the invisible God. Not an introverted form of meditation, but rather a quiet resting that draws you toward a mysterious Other.

What the Jewish philosopher Stein, as yet an unbeliever, can only surmise at the sight of this simple woman at prayer soon becomes for her a certainty: God exists, and in prayer we turn toward him. What an impression it must have made upon the disciples, then, to see Jesus praying quietly for hours, or even all night long! What was it about this remote place, this protracted attention, in silence, to the One whom he calls "Abba"?

"He was praying in a certain place, and when he ceased, one of his disciples said to him, 'Lord, teach us to pray, as John taught his disciples'" (Lk 11:1).

"Teach us to pray." This expresses the yearning to

enter into the realm of this quiet intimacy, this watchful reaching out toward the invisible Presence. Their reverence before the mystery of Jesus' prayer is so great that the disciple does not dare to interrupt the Lord, to "burst in" on his prayer with his question. He waits until Jesus himself comes out of prayer. Only then does he dare to ask, to plead, "Teach us to pray!"

Is it not touching when we come into church and find someone praying quietly there? Does this sight not arouse a yearning to pray? Do we hear in these moments the murmuring of the spring that calls us to the living water? As Ignatius of Antioch, who was martyred around A.D. 110, writes: "There is living water in me, water that murmurs and says within me: Come to the Father" (*Ad Rom.*, 7, 2).

Yearning for prayer is the enticement of the Holy Spirit in us, who draws us to the Father. Indeed, this yearning is already prayer; it is already the prayer of the Spirit of Christ in us.

"Trouble is not the only thing that teaches us to pray"

"For me, prayer is a surge of the heart; it is a simple look turned toward heaven, it is a cry of recognition and of love, embracing both trial and joy." The fourth part of the *Catechism*, on prayer, begins with this quotation from the Little Flower, Saint Thérèse of Lisieux (*Manuscrits autobiographiques*, C 25r).

"A surge of the heart"—that is how Thérèse, whom the Holy Father presented to us as a Doctor of the Church on October 19, 1997, describes the "source of prayer": the heart. "In naming the source of prayer, Scripture speaks sometimes of the soul or the spirit, but most often of the heart (more than a thousand times). . . . It is the *heart* that prays. If our heart is far from God, the words of prayer are in vain" (CCC 2562).

How does the heart manage to "surge"? A folk saying puts it this way: "Trouble teaches us to pray." And so it often does. How many prayers—in our churches, at places of pilgrimage, or wherever—ascend to God from the depths of distress! "Out of the depths I cry to you, O Lord! Lord, hear my voice!" (Ps 130:1–2). If we could hear the prayers that are said day in, day out by those who light a candle before the Maria-Pocs icon in Saint Stephen's Cathedral [in Vienna], we would no doubt become acquainted with every sort of distress imaginable.

But trouble alone does not necessarily teach us to pray. It can also lead to a hardening of the heart. Only that trouble which helps us to recognize and accept the fact that we need God leads us to prayer. Once we recognize, or at least begin to suspect, that we are beggars before God (CCC 2559), that in and of ourselves we are feeble and helpless, then our heart becomes open to prayer. As long as we think that we "don't need God" and have everything under control, our heart is closed.

Does that mean that God wants to make us as small as possible, so as to be the great God himself? Is God pleased to see us in misery? Does God want to see us as slaves, oppressed and powerless?

Prayer comes not only from trouble. Thérèse says that it is a "cry of recognition and of love, embracing both trial and joy". Gratitude, also, teaches us to pray, and even more so—love. Someone who is grateful has an open heart, which humbly acknowledges that everything in our lives is a gift, the trials and the joys. The psalms teach us the outlook of gratitude in all situations of life.

God does not want to "take us down a peg"; in fact, he wants to give us everything, especially himself. He knocks on our door and asks to be admitted (cf. Rev 3:20). Just as Jesus asked the woman at Jacob's well, "Give me a drink" (Jn 4:7), so too he asks us for our heart. He knocks at the door of every human being; he asks each one to let him in. Often it takes the experience of some trouble in order for us to hear God knocking. Does God therefore want us to be in trouble? Should we not rather say: He allows it but does not abandon us to it? Yes, this is what many have experienced: Trouble taught them to pray (again). In their trouble they found God (again). Thus trouble became a blessing. And gratitude rises up in the midst of trial and in the midst of joy.

4

The loss of prayer

Why are we so often afraid of prayer? To be sure, sometimes we are drawn to prayer; sometimes it is like an oasis to be able to rest in prayer. Very often, though, we find that every possible and impossible distraction demands our attention the moment we want to take some time to pray. Then all at once everything else is more important, and we find that we simply do not have time to pray.

Let us try for a moment to understand why these two things happen, yearning for prayer, but also avoiding prayer. Of course the most profound reason why there is in us a yearning to pray is that God calls every person. In every human heart this call is present, faintly or clearly, obscurely or plainly. Prayer is an encounter with God, and God wants to encounter every man. Even before a child begins to say his first prayers, God is already present in his life, and he will remain so, as long as the child's path through life lasts, until his final hour on earth.

This presence of God in every human life is something so great, so basic, that we must constantly ponder it anew, because in the hubbub of everyday routine we forget it all too easily. We profess that God is "all-present", in all things, in all living creatures, but especially in man. For all things, all living creatures, all human beings have their foundation in God: "For 'in him we live and move and have our being'" (Acts 17:28). He holds everything in being, gives life to all; nothing falls from his hand. That is why constantly pondering anew the "omnipresence" of God is so basic for our personal path of prayer.

Yet it also happens that people avoid prayer. How does this come about? What is the most deep-seated reason for this flight from prayer, the encounter with God? The Bible puts us on the right track: In the beginning, in the original state, man lived in great intimacy with God. "Paradise" was the condition of untroubled friendship with God. We can have only a glimmering of what this was like, especially from the experience of yearning for such intimacy with God. The story of original sin and the Fall explains why not only the yearning for God but also the flight from God are found in the human heart.

After the Fall, according to Genesis 3:8, man hides from God, who draws near to him "among the trees of the garden". "I heard the sound of you in the garden, and I was afraid, because I was naked; and I hid myself" (Gen 3:10).

How often since then has our behavior toward God been determined by fear and flight. Sin sows in our hearts the suspicion that God does not mean well with us. Distrust of God runs deep in us, combined with distrust of each other and of ourselves. Yet God's way is different. He calls to us, as he did to our first parents: Adam, "where are you?"—Eve, "what is this that you have done?" (Gen 3:9, 13). "God's sorrowful call to his first children" (CCC 2568) pursues us lovingly and patiently as long as we live, not as an accusation, but rather as an invitation to the intimate friendship of prayer.

5

Prayer in the Old Testament: Abraham's path

When God calls him, Abraham goes forth "as the Lord had told him" (Gen 12:4); Abraham's heart is entirely submissive to the Word and so he obeys. Such attentiveness of the heart, whose decisions are made according to God's will, is essential to prayer, while the words used count only in relation to it. Abraham's prayer is expressed first by deeds: a man of silence, he constructs an altar to the Lord at each stage of his journey. (CCC 2570)

God calls each of us, not only Abraham. But do we listen as Abraham did to God's constant call? And do we also obey immediately? Silently, but with interior animation?

Every one of us knows this urgency within the heart, when we feel that God wants something from us. Something quite specific.

But is it not often the case that, at the very moment when we ought to do something that is absolutely essential and important, we lose ourselves instead in what is unsubstantial, in meaningless details?

It is interesting for us that Abraham, upon whom God bestowed so many promises—and who had to wait an incredibly long time in faith and trust until they were fulfilled—made sure to undertake all that he did in complete union with God.

That is why, wherever he went, he first built an altar to the Lord. A place, that is, where he could be entirely at God's disposal. Because God was the most important thing in his life.

And where should we build this altar? An altar for our prayer, our worship and sacrifice? The best place is our heart.

We do well to build an altar for God in our heart—better yet, to make out of our heart an altar, upon which we can offer to God our sacrifice, our devotion, perhaps also the dedication of our own life: "I am all yours—I belong entirely to you, and I will do only what you will, O Lord."

Perhaps many will not succeed immediately at this total dedication; indeed, it may even evoke inner resistance: What about my own free will?

But God has patience with us. And so he waits until, by and by, we grow into the realization of a particular task in life that he assigns to us; until we recognize the real meaning of our life, that its most noble purpose is to be there for God.

Our conversation with God is a part of this, too. Prayer is often—and surely this is a sign of progress in prayer—a conversation with God. Even Abraham spoke with God.

When the Lord communicated to Abraham in a vision that he himself would be his shield and that his reward would be very great, Abraham asked him: "O Lord GOD, what will you give me, for I continue childless?" (cf. Gen 15:2).

And the Lord answered him: "Look toward heaven, and number the stars, if you are able to number them. . . . So shall your descendants be" (Gen 15:5).

Abraham believed in this promise but asked the Lord again and again, in faith and trust, how to proceed.

Let us, too, always ask the Lord what he expects of us and how to go on. Especially when we find ourselves in seemingly hopeless situations. Then we may even "cry out" to the Lord: Lord, help me, what should I do?

God hears us. He answers our cry. To each of us, then, he gives a sense of what we should do and the inner certainty: This is how I must act now, this way and no other. This is God's will, and not my own whim.

6

Abraham—the father of those who pray

On every page of the Old Testament we encounter prayer. God speaks to men; men answer God. This begins as early as the creation of man, which springs from a "conversation within God": "Then God said, 'Let us make man in our image, after our likeness'" (Gen 1:26). To no other creature does God speak. He creates human beings, and they are. The account continues: "God blessed them, and God said to them, 'Be fruitful and multiply'" (Gen 1:28). The distinguishing mark, the defining characteristic of man is that he can pray, that is, speak with God. Even sin does not break off this conversation: Adam, "where are you?" Eve, "what is this that you have done?" (Gen 3:9, 13). Thus God sorrowfully calls to his first children (CCC 2568). And this conversation never falls mute; rather, it prepares the way of man through all the dramatic events of history. In prayer the people of the Old Testament seek God's direction; in prayer they find and hear God's Word and struggle to obey it.

It would be a long and gripping course of meditations if we were to go through the entire Old Testament as a book about men of prayer, as a school of prayer. We have meditated on Abraham's prayer, his listening to God's direction. Much more could be said about his prayer: his bold intercession for the people of Sodom and Gomorrah (Gen 18:16–33), but especially his readiness to offer up to

God Isaac, the sole bearer of the promise. The conversation between God and Abraham about this incomprehensibly difficult sacrifice is, in its sobriety, the archetype of a prayer of submission in the most difficult hours (cf. Gen 22; CCC 2572). Abraham does, without a lot of talk, what Jesus taught us to pray for: "Thy will be done, on earth as it is in heaven."

The story of Abraham shows, furthermore, that the act of obedience to God is part of prayer. Abraham hears God's appeal and carries it out, too. His answer is not just words, but deeds: "Go from your country"—"So Abram went" (Gen 12:1, 4). "Take your son . . . and offer him . . . as a burnt offering. . . . So Abraham rose early in the morning" (Gen 22:2–3).

Abraham is in yet another respect the great biblical model of the man of prayer: The agreement of word and deed in his life results from his outlook of *faith*, on account of which Abraham is described as the father of all who would come after him. "Abraham believed God, and it was reckoned to him as righteousness" (Rom 4:3). "By faith Abraham obeyed when he was called" (Heb 11:8). The link between word and deed is faith, which puts complete trust in the word and the (interior or exterior) direction of God. Abraham "considered that God was able to raise men even from the dead" (Heb 11:19). The soil in which prayer grows is faith. The man of prayer Abraham, therefore, is known as the "father of believers".

7

Jacob, Joseph, Moses—
men become men of prayer

To read the Old Testament as a school of prayer: our short meditations can only extend the invitation but scarcely accomplish it. We would have to go through the Old Testament page by page in order to trace in detail the paths of prayer. There would be much more to say about Abraham, much about Isaac, but especially about Jacob, who is also called Israel, or one who has "striven with God" (Gen 32:29), because he wrestled all night with God. This nocturnal struggle with God became the prototype of steadfast, constant prayer that does not let God go until he gives his blessing (CCC 2573).

But another scene from the life of Jacob also became one of the prototypes of prayer: the vision by night of the "ladder to heaven" on which the angels of God are ascending and descending. He called the place of this encounter with God Beth-El (house of God), and even today we read this passage on the feast of the dedication of a church: "Surely the Lord is in this place" (Gen 28:16)—an enduring expression of reverence for God's holy presence.

How much could be said about the story of Joseph (Gen 37—50)! In it no prayer of Joseph is recorded for us. On the other hand, the "unbroken thread" of God's providence is that much more evident. In everything that happens to Joseph and in all that he does, God's gracious hand is revealed. Joseph's brothers, who did him harm, through a sorrowful turn of events experience heartfelt repentance and remorse for their wicked deed and finally discover that God works in all things for the good. "Fear not," says Joseph to them—their brother, whom they sold, but who thereby becomes the one who rescues them—"You meant evil against me; but God meant it for good" (Gen 50:19–20; cf. CCC 312).

Among all the men of prayer of the Old Testament, Moses is preeminent. With no other man did God speak thus face to face (Ex 33:11). This intimacy developed slowly; it required preparation. According to one Jewish tradition, the life of Moses proceeded in three stages of forty years each. For the first forty years he lived at Pharaoh's court, as the foster son of the ruler's daughter. He "was instructed in all the wisdom of the Egyptians, and he was mighty in his words and deeds" (Acts 7:22). When he became aware of the distress and misery of his own people and wanted to help them, it resulted in a deadly blow to an Egyptian slave-driver. Moses had to flee. For forty years he lived as an alien in Midian, in the desert. After this long time of preparation—meanwhile he had reached the age of eighty!—God appeared to him in the burning bush, revealed his name to him, and sent him to deliver his people Israel from Egyptian servitude. Finally, the third forty-year period would be taken up by the wandering of God's people in the desert (cf. Acts 7:23–36).

All three stages are, as it were, archetypes of the paths of prayer: the phase of growing up, education, and human accomplishments; then a radical turn that means leaving everything—prestige, knowledge, power—in order to be alone with God in the desert. Finally, the phase of maturity, in which God can place the person completely in his service, with the treasure of experience and knowledge, but also the poverty and the deprivations of the desert period. The life of Moses thus shows us the way to friendship with God, to the goal of all prayer.

Moses stands in the breach

The first conversation with God recorded in the biblical account of Moses is not initiated by him but by God. God calls to him out of the burning bush. He calls to Moses (Ex 3:4) and at the same time makes known to him his calling: "Bring forth my people . . . out of Egypt" (Ex 3:10). The encounter with God in prayer becomes a mission for men. The more God reveals himself to Moses, the more Moses comes to share in God's "perspective". At first he resists the mission from God; he sees his own weaknesses and deficiencies; he is apprehensive about the weight of the impending burden; he tries to evade it. Yet God inspires him with the courage to say Yes: "I will be with you" (Ex 3:12). In this prayerful wrestling with God and with the task he demands from Moses, the latter increasingly becomes God's confidant, involved in his ways and his will (CCC 2575).

Again and again Moses will cry out to God, when he is in great distress, when all seems hopeless. Thus at the very beginning of his mission, when the people are more and more oppressed, his cry for help: "O LORD, why have you done evil to this people? Why did you ever send me?" (Ex 5:22).

When Moses finally can lead the people of Israel out of Egypt, he has the painful experience of watching his people again and again resist their deliverance from slavery in Egypt, because the way through the desert into freedom is hard and long. "Let us alone and let us serve the Egyptians[.] For it would have been better for us to serve the Egyptians than to die in the wilderness" (Ex 14:12).

This desert experience is part of the Christian's path through life. The "old man" in us resists deliverance from slavery to sin. And just as the Israelite people longed for the "fleshpots" of Egypt (Ex 16:3), so too it happens that we look back to the old life that we have left behind. Yet God, through the hand of Moses, releases his people from their old attachment to slavery, so that they may learn to live trusting in God completely. Israel's forty years in the desert, the "Exodus" into the Promised Land, has been viewed since antiquity as the prototype of the path of faith, with all the joys of deliverance and all the trials of this time of testing.

Moses is the great model of the shepherd, the mediator, and the intercessor. He has the privilege of bringing God's ordinances to the people, the Ten Commandments, which God entrusted to him on Mount Sinai (Ex 20:1–21). Yet he also becomes the great intercessor with God, when the people have turned away from God and worshipped the golden calf. In a moving prayer of supplication, Moses offers himself to God as a sacrifice, so that his people may be spared the punishment they have deserved. He would rather be blotted out of the book of life than have the people whom God had told him to rescue be ruined (Ex 32:32; cf. 32:11–14). For his people Moses "stood in the breach" (Ps 106:23)—a foreshadowing of Jesus Christ, who laid down his life for all.

David and his openheartedness to God

The Old Testament has a wealth of scenes that have become "archetypes" of prayer, in which the person praying appears as though in a series of "tableaux". Abraham, Jacob, and Moses have already been named. Other personages should be mentioned, at least as a reference, as an invitation to read about them on one's own.

There is Hannah, the wife of Elkanah, who at the shrine in Shiloh tearfully pours out to God all her sorrow over her childlessness—the archetype of so many women who plaintively turn to God (1 Sam 1:1–18). And there is the same Hannah again, who at the same shrine sings her hymn of thanksgiving to God for Samuel, the child she has obtained from God by her weeping and prayers (1 Sam 1:21—2:11). There is Samuel, the boy who has been consecrated to God, whom the Lord calls for the first time at night while he is asleep; [he answers,] "Speak, LORD, for your servant is listening" (1 Sam 3:9). This is the prototype of a "school of prayer" (cf. CCC 2578), in which the child learns, from the prayer of his mother and with the help of the elderly priest Eli, to listen to God and to speak with him. No wonder this passage is often read when praying for vocations to the priesthood and religious life.

There would be much to say about David. He is a man of action, a shepherd at first, then a military leader, and finally king of all Israel. Many scenes from his life show that his heart is completely open to God. For instance, his joyful dance before the Ark of the Covenant: "It was before the LORD [that I danced]." He, the king, is not ashamed of that, even if Michal, his wife, deems it unworthy of him (2 Sam 6:14–23). For example, his remorse after committing adultery with Bathsheba and murdering her husband, Uriah—archetype of the prayer of contrition: "Have mercy on me, O God, according to your steadfast love; according to your abundant mercy blot out my transgressions. . . . Against you, you only, have I sinned, and done that which is evil in your sight" (Ps 51:1, 4; 2 Sam 12:13). David is considered to be the one who composed and prayed the psalms—even though most of them are from a later date (CCC 2585–89). They testify to how King David lives in the memory of his people as the one who brings every situation in life into prayer: affliction and war, sickness and lamenting, asking, pleading, thanksgiving, praise, jubilation—nothing is kept back from God, not even requests directed against enemies. David, who throughout his life was a man of action, a warrior, was at the same time a man who trusted in God: a radiant example of magnanimity for all who have public responsibilities. This quality makes him so amiable, a king "after God's own heart" (CCC 2579).

The prophets are men of prayer, because they listen to God. Among them all, Elijah is preeminent, the archetype of the "man of God". Here, too, are "archetypes" of prayer: Elijah by the wadi [brook] Cherith—an image of solitude, model of the secluded life of a hermit (1 Kings 17:2–7); Elijah on Mount Carmel—an image of the power of prayer, which calls down God's fire and Spirit (1 Kings 18); Elijah in the desert—the prayer of the disheartened man, who can go no farther and whom God fortifies with bread for the journey (1 Kings 19:1–8); finally, Elijah on the mountain of God, encountering God in the "still, small voice" (1 Kings 19:12). Impressive images of men of prayer, valid for our journey, too.

Jesus, the Man of prayer

Much more could be said about prayer in the Old Testament. We will return later to the book of Psalms, that great collection of one hundred fifty prayers: It has become the nucleus of the Church's treasury of prayer.

We see in Jesus' own prayer how deeply rooted Christian prayer is in Old Testament Jewish prayer. He whom we acknowledge to be the Son of God became man of the Virgin Mary and, as man, learned to pray and prayed with a human heart (CCC 2599).

The mystery of this heart remains unfathomable. It is the human heart of the Son of God (CCC 470). Jesus' innermost secret is his divine oneness with the Father. Yet he experienced this union as a man, too, and that becomes especially clear in his prayer.

Jesus learned to pray from Mary and Joseph, using the forms and expressions of Jewish prayer. In the synagogue he became acquainted with the liturgy of his people; in the Temple in Jerusalem he prayed with the pilgrims from Nazareth. There, however, in the Temple, the deeper, hidden source of his prayer was manifested for the first time. To his parents, who were looking for him anxiously, the twelve-year-old said: "Did you not know that I must be in my Father's house?" (Lk 2:49).

Who is his Father? What does it mean, that he can call God "Abba" (Mk 14:36), "Papa", so matter-of-factly? From this first announcement of his relation to

God, his Father, until the final cry of trust and self-abandonment on the cross: "Father, into your hands I commit my spirit" (Lk 23:46), his entire public life and work are nourished by this hidden source: his oneness with the Father.

The Gospels testify that he frequently goes into seclusion in order to pray, sometimes all night. Many among his followers to this day walk this path and pray especially at night. From these hours of being alone with the Father comes his work, come his words, his preaching, his healings, and ultimately his willingness to walk the way to Jerusalem, to the sorrowful Cross, even to the hour of mortal agony: "Abba, Father! . . . Not what I will, but what you will" (Mk 14:36).

From this oneness in prayer with the Father come also the steps and decisions that lead to the founding of the Church: for example, the selection and sending of the Twelve (Lk 6:12; cf. Mk 3:13–19), his prayer for Peter, that his faith may not fail (Lk 22:32), and above all his prayer that all may be one, "as you, Father, are in me, and I [am] in you" (Jn 17:21).

Jesus, the Teacher of prayer

No one has ever prayed as Jesus did. His prayer is the language of a heart that is the human heart of the Son of God. Jesus' prayer is the "translation" of the "conversation" among the Divine Persons into the form of human praying. If we want to have some idea of what makes Jesus' prayer so incomparable, we must immerse ourselves in the deepest, most magnificent mystery of the faith: that God is the triune, the One God—Father, Son, and Holy Spirit—communion in unity, endless exchange of love: "God is love" (1 Jn 4:8). Out of this depth comes Jesus' prayer.

No man has ever fathomed this depth. But all men are invited to enter into it, to have a share in Jesus' prayer. He wants us all to find our way to the Father through him. When Jesus teaches his disciples to pray, he takes them by the hand, so to speak, in order to lead them to the Father, into the life of the living God.

He does this first by his own example. To see Jesus praying was the first school of prayer for his disciples. His prayer awakened in them a new longing to learn to pray themselves. The experience shows us how important a living example is in leading others onto the path of prayer. It opens up a willingness in the heart to perceive the interior call from God and to respond to the Holy Spirit's urging with personal prayer. In order for the heart to become open to God's call, to become a responsive, praying heart, it must be ready: "My heart is ready, O God, my heart is ready [Douay-Rheims]; I will sing and make melody [RSV]", the Psalmist sings (Ps 57:7). When the heart becomes hardened, it cannot follow Jesus on the path of his prayer (cf. Mk 3:5–6).

Jesus' school of prayer consists first of all in imitation. Before he teaches his disciples to pray, he impresses upon them the attitudes that are decisive for his life: the Beatitudes (Mt 5:3–12). Whoever is poor in spirit, merciful and peace-loving, meek and pure of heart, as Jesus demonstrated by his life, will also be able to pray like Jesus. Someone who forgives as Jesus did, pardoning even those who persecute him unjustly, who are his enemies (cf. Mt 5:44–47) and want to kill him, his heart will learn to pray as the heart of Jesus prayed.

By inviting us to be perfect "as your heavenly Father is perfect" (Mt 5:48)—that is, to be perfect as he, Jesus, is perfect—he awakens in us the yearning to become like him. There are two possible reactions to this invitation: either to be discouraged in light of our own weakness and to "go away sorrowful" (cf. Mt 19:22), or else to ask Jesus to lead us where we ourselves cannot go by our own strength. From this response, then, also comes the request that the Lord might teach us how to pray. Thus we pray for the ability to pray, because Jesus has enkindled in us the desire, the will to pray, and also because we see how little we can do on our own. The mere longing for it becomes a prayer: "Lord, teach us to pray" (Lk 11:1).

Childlike trust is the attitude that Jesus wants to bestow upon us as the posture of prayer. Jesus finds this trust, this faith, especially among the poor and the foreigners, while he is saddened by the little faith of his own disciples (CCC 2610). So that they might really learn to pray, with his heart, so to speak, he will send to them, and to us all, his Holy Spirit, who despite our weakness prays in us, "according to the will of God" (cf. Rom 8:15–16, 26–27).

Praying to Jesus

Something entirely new and unprecedented: Not only does Jesus himself pray, not only does Jesus teach others to pray, but prayer is addressed to him as well. Even though the prayer of the Church is addressed in the first place to God the Father, there have been prayers addressed to Jesus ever since the earliest period (CCC 2665), starting with the yearning call for the coming of the Lord ("Maranatha", 1 Cor 16:22) and the simple *Kyrie eleison*, "Lord, have mercy". If Jesus were a mere man, if he were not true God and true man, we would not be permitted to pray to him. He could be, at most, the model for our prayer. Many of our prayers, especially the very personal ones, are directed to Jesus, the Redeemer, the Savior. Think, for instance, of the "Jesus Prayer" customary in the Eastern Church: "Lord Jesus Christ, Son of God, have mercy on me, a sinner [Mt 9:27; Mk 10:48]" (CCC 2616). It is a well-established practice of prayer in the Eastern Church to repeat this short prayer over and over again until it becomes the continual prayer of the heart, so as to carry out the word and will of Jesus that we should pray at all times unceasingly (cf. Lk 18:1).

An example of turning confidently to Jesus is provided by the many people whom we meet in the Gospels coming to Jesus with requests. When Jesus grants these requests, which often arise from great distress, this already manifests who he is and what a mystery is concealed and at the same time revealed in his person. The people who make their way through the crowd to Jesus with their sick relatives, or with their own sufferings, to ask him for healing turn to Jesus the man—for instance, the blind men who call to Jesus, "Have mercy on us, Son of David!" (cf. Mk 10:48). Perhaps they suspect and hope that Jesus is the promised Messiah who will free them from all misery. Yet they encounter more than a man. When Jesus says to the crippled man who has been let down at his feet through the roof, "My son, your sins are forgiven" (Mk 2:5), some say, "It is blasphemy! Who can forgive sins but God alone?" (Mk 2:7).

Only God can forgive sins. As though guided by a sure instinct, people turn to Jesus and ask him for his mercy, the mercy of God, which becomes present in his forgiving words, his healing deeds.

Ever since Pentecost, since the descent of the Holy Spirit, this Divine Person urges hearts to approach Jesus as confidently as people did during his earthly life—to confide completely in Jesus, as we can do only in a trusting relationship with God. The prayer of the Apostle Thomas, when he touched the marks of Jesus' wounds, became the epitome of prayer addressed to Jesus: "My Lord and my God!" (Jn 20:28). And yet, when we worship Jesus lovingly in this way, our prayer is still always addressed to God the Father "through Jesus Christ" (cf. Rom 1:8; Eph 2:18).

Mary—the woman of prayer who intercedes

Jesus' prayer is incomparable: it is his intimate oneness with the Father. Yet Jesus' prayer should become our prayer, because his Father becomes our Father, because through Jesus we receive the Spirit "who makes us children of God".

In the New Testament, consequently, there is a new kind of prayer, different from and greater than all the longing of the human heart that finds expression in the prayer of all religions. This new prayer, which the Holy Spirit places in our hearts, begins in the creature who is called "the dawn of the new creation". Mary is the first woman of this new prayer, in whom the Holy Spirit can work completely unimpeded. Because she is "full of grace", her prayer is full, complete devotion to God. So full of trust, so full of the Holy Spirit should our prayer become also: the prayer of the children of God (CCC 2617).

The Little Flower, Saint Thérèse, who had a great love for Mary (the smile of Mary healed her as a child), vehemently resisted the idea that Mary should be carried off to unreachable heights: "How I would have loved to be a priest in order to preach about the Blessed Virgin! One sermon would be sufficient to say everything I think about this subject. I'd first make people understand how little is known by us about her life. We shouldn't say unlikely things or things we don't know anything about!", she writes. And Thérèse clarifies what she means: "I'm sure that her real life was very simple. They show her to us as unapproachable, but they should present her as imitable, bringing out her virtues, saying that she lived by faith just like ourselves." [1]

In the last poem Thérèse wrote (it is also the longest), she meditates on Mary's life, her sorrows, her prayer: "In pondering *your life in the holy Gospels,* / I dare look at you and come near you. / It's not difficult for me to believe I'm your child, / For I see you human and suffering like me." [2]

Because Mary is so simple, the "little ones" can take her not only as an example for the "Little Way", but also as their helper and intercessor, in short, as their mother. "Mother full of grace, I know that in Nazareth / You live in poverty, wanting nothing more. / *No rapture, miracle, or ecstasy / Embellish your life, O Queen of the Elect!* . . . / The number of little ones on earth is truly great. / They can raise their eyes to you without trembling. / It's by *the ordinary way,* incomparable Mother, / That you like to walk, to guide them to Heaven" (From the poem "Why I Love You, O Mary"). [3]

How comforting it is to read, then, that the little Saint of Lisieux found it difficult to pray the Rosary. Try as she might, she could scarcely recollect herself. That distressed her, until she placed her trust completely in

[1] Saint Thérèse of Lisieux, *Her Last Conversations,* trans. John Clarke (Washington, D.C.: Institute of Carmelite Studies, 1977), p. 161.

[2] *The Poetry of Saint Thérèse of Lisieux,* trans. Donald Kinney (Washington, D.C.: Institute of Carmelite Studies, 1996), p. 215.

[3] Ibid., p. 218.

Mary's poverty of spirit: "I think that the Queen of Heaven, as my mother, will see my good intention and be satisfied with that."

Prayer of petition—
the rudimentary form of human prayer

The Church makes its first appearance praying. With one accord devoted to prayer, the primordial Church waits for the coming of the promised Spirit (Acts 1:14). We see the first community of Jerusalem at prayer (Acts 2:42; 12:5). It still lives entirely in the world of Jewish prayer (Acts 3:1), but very soon Christian prayer finds its own forms of expression, without leaving the Israelite soil in which it is rooted. The Old Testament remains the great school of prayer for the Church. All the prayer forms of the Old Covenant are seen anew in the light of Christ, are further developed under the influence of the Holy Spirit. First and foremost there is the prayer of petition. This is the primordial form of human prayer, not only in the Old Testament, but probably in all religions. Jesus himself teaches the disciples, who ask him for instructions in prayer, to make the seven petitions of the Our Father.

Asking God for things is the expression of our dependence. As creatures we rely in everything on him, from whom we have everything, in whom we live and move and have our being (Acts 17:28). In the prayer of petition we acknowledge our neediness and God's greatness. When we ask God for something, we give him honor, which is why a prayer of petition also contains an element of adoration.

Often prayers of petition may appear to "incapacitate" man. The autonomous man does not want to have to ask for anything, feels that it is humiliating to get in line with petitioners. Behind this attitude there is a twofold miscalculation: a failure to recognize human neediness (that we, as human beings, depend on one another as well and hence owe it to each other to say "Please" and "Thank you") and a failure to appreciate God's greatness, which is not manifested in God's making us feel the most bitter kind of dependence possible. Rather, the main thing that Jesus teaches us in prayers of petition is a limitless trust in the One whom we, with him, are privileged to call "Abba", Father.

To ask God with childlike confidence for everything we need does not incapacitate us but rather bestows on us the incomparable dignity of being children of God, of having friendship with God.

That is why Jesus also teaches us to knock constantly and urgently on God's door, like an importunate friend (Lk 11:5–13; CCC 2613).

Often, therefore, the prayer of petition is the beginning of the turning back to God (CCC 2629). A predicament teaches us, as it taught the prodigal son, to remember the One whom we are forgetting, whose gifts we have ungratefully taken for granted and carelessly squandered. If in this predicament we get up and set out again and return to God, asking for his forgiveness and his help, then we will discover that it is not a stern judge who awaits us, but a loving Father (cf. Lk 15:11–32).

15

" . . . And you will be a blessing"

If the prayer of petition is the basic form of prayer, then blessing is its "basic movement" (CCC 2626). In what sense? In order to understand the "twofold movement" of blessing in the biblical sense, we must first point out a linguistic peculiarity. In Hebrew, one and the same word designates the blessing that proceeds from God and the prayerful, grateful response of man: *barak*, *benedicere*, as it is translated into Latin.

Every blessing comes from God: "Blessing is a divine and life-giving action, the source of which is the Father" (CCC 1078). God's greatest blessing is his own Son, "the blessed fruit of thy womb", as we pray in the Hail Mary.

When men encounter God's good deeds, when they become aware of his blessings and share in them, there follows as the suitable response, so to speak, a grateful return of this blessing to God. So we read at the beginning of the great hymn of blessing in the Letter to the Ephesians: "Blessed be the God and Father of our Lord Jesus Christ, who has blessed us in Christ with every spiritual blessing in the heavenly places" (Eph 1:3).

"From the beginning until the end of time the whole of God's work is a *blessing*"; the Bible sees God's whole plan of salvation "as one vast divine blessing" (CCC 1079). That is why all prayer, whether petition or thanksgiving, praise or adoration, is a human response that "blesses" God. The *Benedictus*, Zechariah's canticle of praise (Lk 1:68–79), and Mary's song of praise, the *Magnificat* (Lk 1:46–55), are "blessings" of this type, singing praise to God for His graces.

The one whom God blesses should himself become a blessing. Abraham, who accepted God's call and blessing in faith, for this reason hears the promise: "You will be a blessing. . . . [B]y you all the families of the earth shall bless themselves" (Gen 12:2–3). A spiritual master and mother of our day, Julia Verhaeghe, says accordingly: "We must be a blessing. That is our duty." We can be a blessing especially by blessing others, even our enemies: "Bless those who persecute you; bless and do not curse them" (Rom 12:14). The many blessings of the Church, those given in public as well as the ones at home in the family, are a means of obtaining God's blessing and protection (for instance, the sign of the cross marked on the forehead of a child who is going away from home), as well as a way of returning thanks to God who is blessed, from whom all blessings flow, so that all things may return to him blessed and fulfilled, whole and holy.

16

Adoration

"Begone, Satan! for it is written, 'You shall worship the Lord your God and him only shall you serve'" (Mt 4:10). Thus Jesus rejects the tempter's arrogant claim that he would give him all the kingdoms of the world, "if you will fall down and worship me" (Mt 4:9).

Man should not prostrate himself in worship before any creature. We may adore God alone; rendering adoration to a creature is idolatry. But what is adoration? What place does it have in the world of prayer? What is its origin; how does it manifest itself, in the heart and outwardly?

Let us begin with bodily expressions. Everywhere in the Bible we encounter the gesture of prostration as an expression of adoration: It is intended for God alone, or for those who embody God's presence, for instance, the three guests, the messengers of God who visit Abraham (cf. Gen 18:2). In the book of Revelation, God is adored in the "heavenly liturgy" by means of this gesture: "The twenty-four elders fall down before him who is seated on the throne and worship him" (Rev 4:10). This gesture is familiar to Islam. I see in front of me a Muslim who, in the middle of the airport in Rome, spreads out his prayer rug and prostrates himself in prayer.

Is this posture not too "subservient" for Christians? Have we not been liberated by Christ, so as to walk upright in freedom as sons and daughters of God, no longer groveling as slaves? Many Christians think that it is no longer fitting for us to kneel, since we have been raised by Jesus' Resurrection to a form of prayer that stands upright.

Certainly adoration of God is not necessarily connected with the bodily posture of bending the knee. And yet this posture suits this type of prayer. "*Adoration* is the first attitude of man acknowledging that he is a creature before his Creator" (CCC 2628). To fall prostrate before God in no way diminishes man: "Adoration of the thrice-holy and sovereign God of love blends with humility and gives assurance to our supplications" (ibid.). Someone who casts himself down in adoration before God, and only before him, is in no danger of prostrating himself before the many idols that enslave man and blind him.

Many eyewitnesses have spoken of the unforgettable impression made on them by the sight of the saintly Curé of Ars kneeling before the tabernacle in adoration. Just as the man born blind, who was healed, believed and prostrated himself in worship before Jesus (cf. Jn 9:38), so also love for our Savior, who is present in the Eucharist, urges us to adore him in silence.

Adoration: this is the interior and exterior attitude toward him at whose name "every knee should bow, in heaven and on earth and under the earth" (Phil 2:10): Jesus Christ, the Lord.

17

Praise

Psalm 22, which Jesus prayed on the Cross ("My God, my God, why have you forsaken me?"), says: "Yet you are holy, enthroned on the praises of Israel" (Ps 22:3)— that, at least, is one possible reading of this verse. God is enthroned on or, as it is also translated, dwells in the praise of Israel. What does this expression mean, which is found immediately after the great lament that God has abandoned the suffering man who is praying?

It is an exquisite testimony to the experience of the People of God in prayer: even in the most dire need, in the most severe affliction, even in the night of abandonment by God, the praise of God is not silenced. And this is precisely how people who pray experience God's nearness, for he "dwells in the praise of Israel". "In you our fathers trusted; they trusted, and you did deliver them. To you they cried, and were saved" (Ps 22:4–5).

"Praise is the form of prayer which recognizes most immediately that God is God" (CCC 2639). There can be various occasions for praising God: joy at receiving his help, the gift of a special grace, gratitude for being rescued from dangers, and many other reasons. Yet the basis for praising God is always God himself: "[Praise] lauds God for his own sake and gives him glory, quite beyond what he does, but simply because HE IS" (CCC 2639).

Our [Austrian Catholic] hymnbook is entitled *Gotteslob* [Praise of God]. All forms of expressing prayer in song are summed up in the notion of "praise of God". For in all forms of prayer, in petition and thanksgiving, blessing and intercession, the recognition of God for his own sake is always included. In praise it finds its purest form of expression. Therefore the praise of God should always have a central place in our prayer. The Church's Morning Prayer was traditionally called "Lauds", [from the Latin word] meaning "the praises", because the day ought to begin with the praise of God. Evening Prayer, also (to which Psalm 22 belongs in the Jewish liturgy), is characterized by the praise of God. Unceasingly the praise of God resounds in the Church. It finds its highest, most perfect expression in the Eucharist, the "sacrifice of praise" that is offered to God all over the world (CCC 2643), "from East to West" (Third Eucharistic Prayer).

The praise of God is bound up with no particular place; it can arise from our hearts everywhere. True, genuine praise of God comes from love, which rejoices in God. A loving heart wants to praise, and conversely, through the praise of God, love grows as well: "Sing and make melody with all your heart in praise of the Lord" (cf. Eph 5:19). Thus the praise of God drives away ill-humor, pettiness, bitterness. The heart is widened and grows in trust. We learn, as Israel once did, that God really dwells in the praise of his people. Heaven opens a little bit—the place where the praise of God is without end, because God's glory is seen unveiled.

18

Thanksgiving

"With joy, give thanks to the Father" (cf. Col 1:12). Thanks, thanksgiving, thankfulness should be part of every Christian prayer. When the Apostle Paul speaks of giving thanks, and he does so very often (thirty-four times), the tone is always jubilant. It is as if he could never tire of thanking God constantly for everything in all situations. He invites all to give thanks at all times. All that we do, and all that we suffer, too, is as though transformed by thanksgiving and acquires an undertone of joy.

What brings about an attitude of thankfulness, the practice of continual thanksgiving? In Paul's case, his own experience, which changed and transformed his whole life, caused an inexhaustible spring of thanksgiving to flow from within him: "With joy, [give] thanks to the Father, who has qualified us to share in the inheritance of the saints in light. He has delivered us from the dominion of darkness and transferred us to the kingdom of his beloved Son, in whom we have redemption, the forgiveness of sins" (Col 1:12–14).

What Paul experienced for himself makes him forever grateful: his deliverance, his encounter with Jesus Christ. Since that time he knows that he can only give thanks, at every moment, in all situations, and for everything. And that is why he encourages constant thankfulness: "Give thanks in all circumstances; for this is the will of God in Christ Jesus for you" (1 Thess 5:18).

Thanks are due in the first place to God; since everything is his gift, since all good things come from him, the proper response is thanks. "Just as *eulogein* (praise, blessing) is man's response to God's *eulogia* (blessing), so too is *charis, eucharistia* (thanksgiving) the response to God's *charis* (grace, favor)", writes Auxiliary Bishop Alois Stöger (d. 1999) (in the article "Dank" [Thanksgiving], in the *Bibeltheologisches Wörterbuch* [Theological dictionary of the Bible]). "In thanksgiving a return is made to God of that which he himself has given" (ibid.).

Ingratitude is, according to Paul, one of the vices of men "in the last days" (2 Tim 3:2). It poisons life completely, making it gray and joyless. It blinds a person to the good and paralyzes prayer. So it becomes even clearer that the ability to thank is itself a grace, a present. That is why we should strive for thankfulness, ask for it, and receive it as God's gift, which gives us reason to thank again.

The deepest root of the prayer of Christian thanksgiving is Jesus' thanks to his Father. All that he has, his whole life, he has from him, thanks to him. We are drawn into his prayer of thanksgiving (*eucharistia*) to the Father especially by the celebration of the Eucharist, in which we thank God the Father for everything with, through, and in Christ (CCC 2637). We should pray for and also celebrate this fundamental orientation of our prayer—radiant, joyous thankfulness—in every Eucharist. Let us pray for the ability to give thanks!

19

Intercession

Adoration, praise and thanksgiving, blessing and petition: these are the forms of prayer that we have looked at briefly so far. The prayer of intercession is discussed in the *Catechism* (CCC 2634–36) as a separate form of prayer.

Our "school of prayer" looks primarily to Jesus. He is our "prayer leader"; again and again we return to his prayer to the Father, in the case of intercessory prayer as well. The archetype and source of our own intercession is Jesus, our "advocate" with the Father (1 Jn 2:1). Jesus did not pray to the Father merely as a contemplative worshipper; he makes intercession to the Father for his own, for us. So he says to Peter: "Simon, Simon, behold, Satan demanded to have you, that he might sift you like wheat, but I have prayed for you that your faith may not fail" (Lk 22:31–32). Jesus' intercession for Peter is to this day the guarantee that Peter, in his successor, will remain firm and unshakeable in his faith. Jesus prayed not only for Peter but for all his disciples when he addressed his great high-priestly prayer (Jn 17) to the Father: "I am praying for them; I am not praying for the world but for those whom you have given me" (Jn 17:9).

We cannot meditate enough upon what it means that Jesus is our Intercessor, that he never stops interceding for us with the Father: "But if any one does sin, we have an advocate [intercessor: Paraclete] with the Father, Jesus Christ the righteous; and he is the expiation for our sins, and not for ours only but also for the sins of the whole world" (1 Jn 2:1–2). Jesus is therefore our Intercessor, not only by his petitions, but also by reason of his entire life, which he offered "for our sins" as "expiation". In the "farewell prayer" in the Cenacle, the Lord explains how he accomplishes his intercession: "For their sake I consecrate myself, that they also may be consecrated in truth" (Jn 17:19). He "consecrates himself for us" in that he lays down and sacrifices his life for us: that is his great prayer of intercession for us. And he remains forever in this sacrifice for us: "Consequently he is able for all time to save those who draw near to God through him, since he always lives to make intercession for them" (Heb 7:25).

When we—strengthened by the "other Counselor" (Jn 14:16) or Advocate that Jesus has sent to us, the Holy Spirit—make intercession, then we unite ourselves with Jesus' intercession for all mankind. How "well received" our intercession is with the Father depends on whether our prayer of intercession is united with Jesus' prayer, thereby attaining the breadth and depth of his self-offering for all mankind. That is why the Church, too, in her prayer of intercession, prays "for all men" (1 Tim 2:1), even for her enemies and persecutors, and also "for the salvation of those who reject the Gospel".

20

Prayer must be learned

We have examined several forms in which Christian prayer unfolds. We turn now to the living sources from which prayer flows, or, more precisely, on which prayer can draw. For it is the same with prayer as with doing good: we all have the natural inclination for it, and somewhere in every human being slumbers or stirs the yearning both to do good and also to pray. Yet in order to do good concretely, we then need to will it, to make a decision and actually accomplish it. It is no different with prayer: "One must have the will to pray" (CCC 2650). It is not enough to wait for prayer to burst forth spontaneously in my heart, to wait until I feel like praying or happen to have time for it. I must will it and struggle so that I actually do it. I must take the time for it, because the time is not going to show up by chance. I must practice praying, just as I practice doing good deeds, which, when done repeatedly, become a virtue, that is, a "good habit", which makes me ready to do good promptly, which turns doing good into something that I need to do and enjoy doing. Virtues do not come about on their own; they must be learned, acquired with effort, and patiently practiced. There is no really human life without them. Someone who merely follows his spontaneous impulses eventually becomes the slave of his desires.

"One must also learn how to pray" (CCC 2650). We

say about somebody that he is a "good man", not simply because he occasionally does something good, but rather when he proves to be good in all that he is and does. We call somebody "a person of prayer" when he turns to prayer, not only in the occasional emergency, but when prayer is "interwoven" with all that that person is and does.

It is a marvelous thing to meet people who are completely "steeped" in prayer, whose faces bear the imprint of prayer. Somehow we sense in their presence that the person who prays has become more fully and profoundly human. Let us ask them about the paths of their prayer life, about the sources of their prayer! Let us ask them how they became people of prayer. Not without teachers of prayer! Not without the interior Teacher, the Holy Spirit, who "helps us in our weakness" and intercedes for us (Rom 8:26–27). Furthermore, not without the living transmission of prayer through the Church, through her "tradition of Christian prayer" (CCC 2651). The Church teaches us to pray through various ways of handing on the tradition: through our first "teachers" of prayer, usually parents; through the liturgical prayer of the Church, which introduces us to the language and the accomplishment of prayer; through particular places and times that are conducive to prayer; but especially through the gifts of faith, hope, and charity, which are actually the "humus" in which prayer can grow. We will investigate these wellsprings of prayer.

21

Faith, hope, charity: Wellsprings of prayer

We learn the natural, human virtues by doing good repeatedly. As for the "theological virtues"—faith, hope, charity—we can open or close ourselves to them. We cannot "acquire" them on our own. They are gifts of God, gifts of his love, which we can ask for but cannot "make" by ourselves. In our prayer life we can gain much by practicing, and to that extent we can learn to pray on our own. Yet we cannot make the deepest wellsprings of our prayer flow by our own power. God himself makes them burst forth. The Holy Spirit, through whom God's love is poured into our hearts (cf. Rom 5:5), becomes in us the living source of prayer. As important, as indispensable as the "natural" preparations for prayer are (recollection, an upright life, suitable times and places, practical helps), they still do not "produce" Christian prayer. As helpful as methods of meditation, of quieting and emptying oneself, of making progress in prayer may be, they are still not Christian prayer, nor do they bring it about in and of themselves.

Christian prayer is the expression of divine life in us; it springs from the virtues that we call "theological", because they are completely and absolutely the gifts of God and unite us with him, indeed, make us one with him. The door, the "narrow gate" (CCC 2656) to prayer is faith. In faith we "touch" God, who is present but invisible. In faith we listen to him, speak to him, his

Word meets with us, and we give an answer. If faith means: "With his whole being man gives his assent to God" (CCC 143), then it is clear that this "Yes" of faith is possible only because God gives us the strength and the grace for it. Prayer lives on this "Yes" of faith. That is why prayer ascends only when it is borne aloft by faith.

Yet it is hope that gives wings to prayer, for hope causes us to be "anchored" with steadfast confidence in God. We do not draw the strength of hope from ourselves, either. God himself grants us the unshakeable trust that he will remain true to his promises.

Now prayer, as Saint Thomas Aquinas says, is "the interpreter of hope". After all, we ask only for what we have good reason to hope for. We try to avoid "vain requests". The greater, the stronger our hope, the more we dare to ask for. And conversely, our prayer strengthens our hope (CCC 2657): the more intimate we become with God (even though he always remains the Incomprehensible, the Mysterious One), the firmer our hope, because charity becomes ever more alive. This is the most profound theological source of prayer: "whoever draws from it reaches the summit of prayer" (CCC 2658), because charity makes us one with him. And what more do we yearn for in prayer than that?

22

Prayer and liturgy

The liturgy is among the principal sources of prayer. It is, as the [Second Vatican] Council says, "the summit toward which the activity of the Church is directed; it is also the font from which all her power flows" (*Sacrosanctum Concilium* 10, quoted in CCC 1074).

Even when we pray all alone, in secret, our prayer is still not isolated. It is always the prayer of the Church as well, whose members we are privileged to be. In our morning and night prayers we are united with all those who begin or end their day with God.

This becomes particularly evident in the Church's "Liturgy of the Hours" (CCC 1174). Even the person who prays Lauds or Vespers [Morning or Evening Prayer] in private, who only says the breviary on his own, is thereby united with the entire community of prayer. It is, after all, "the public prayer of the Church".

These ecclesiastical forms of prayer support and nourish personal prayer. We become familiar with the psalms and learn to pray in their words. From the hymns of the Liturgy of the Hours our prayer gathers images and expressive power. The short excerpts from Scripture, the antiphons, especially if they are repeated often, are imprinted on our memory and can enliven our prayer and become "ejaculatory prayers".

In all this the law of repetition holds, which is an essential part of liturgy. The liturgy cannot be completely new each time; it always requires as well some familiarity with the gestures and words, by which those who pray and celebrate together can orient themselves, and also more easily express themselves collectively and personally.

The liturgy of the Church is therefore one of the most important "schools of prayer". Jesus in his humanity learned to pray, not only at home, but also in the synagogue of Nazareth, in the words and rhythms of the prayer of his people (CCC 2599). Familiarity with the liturgy of the Church, with her Eucharist and her feast days, is for most of us also one of the best paths to prayer.

Acquaintance with liturgical forms can be for us a genuine aid to prayer, but this is true not only of the externals. Above all it is true of what happens interiorly, our "active participation" in the liturgy, which does not necessarily consist of a lot of "activity", but rather in "experiencing" empathetically what is happening in the liturgy.

Prayerful participation in a worship service is supported and often carried by praying and singing in common. Saint Augustine was so moved by the worship service of Saint Ambrose in Milan, by the communal praying and singing of the congregation, that it brought him one big step nearer to his conversion. A worship service, especially the liturgy of the Eucharist, can radiate tremendous power; the most profound reason for this is that Jesus' most characteristic prayer, his thanksgiving (Eucharist) to the Father, becomes truly present here. It depends also, however, on whether and how often we, the celebrating community, concelebrate the liturgy "on the altar of the heart" (cf. CCC 2655), and on how well we prepare for it and allow it to resonate in our personal prayer.

23

The Bible and prayer

Sacred Scripture, no doubt, should be counted in a special way among the "wellsprings of prayer". When we reflect on what the Bible means for our understanding of the faith, we realize to what extent it is one of the sources "where Christ awaits us to enable us to drink of the Holy Spirit" (CCC 2652).

"In Sacred Scripture, the Church constantly finds her nourishment and her strength, for she welcomes it not as a human word, 'but as what it really is, the word of God' [1 Thess 2:13; cf. DV 24]" (CCC 104). So we can say, with the Council, that in the words of the Bible God the Father "comes lovingly to meet his children, and talks with them" (ibid., quoting DV 21).

Since God speaks to us, then, in the words of Sacred Scripture, this requires of us "an understanding mind" (1 Kings 3:9) in order to hear his voice: "O that today you would hearken to his voice! Harden not your hearts, as at Meribah, as on the day at Massah in the wilderness" (Ps 95:7–8).

God speaks to us "in many and various ways" (Heb 1:1): through the language of creation, through events, through the voice of conscience that resounds in man's innermost being (CCC 1776). Therefore, in order to be able to hear Sacred Scripture as the Word of God, prayerful listening to God's manifold speech is necessary: "One who has not yet heard God's voice in his life will not hear it in Sacred Scripture either" (Fr. Augustine K. Fenz, O.Cist.).

Experience proves that "'prayer should accompany the reading of Sacred Scripture, so that a dialogue takes place between God and man. For "we speak to him when we pray; we listen to him when we read the divine oracles"' [*DV* 25, quoting Saint Ambrose, *De officiis ministrorum* 1, 20, 88: PL 16, 50]" (CCC 2653).

It is an unerring sign of a spiritual awakening when yearning for the Word of God increases: "Your words were found, and I ate them, and your words became to me a joy and the delight of my heart" (Jer 15:16). Hunger and thirst for God's Word are signs that the Holy Spirit is moving the heart to seek God and to listen to him. This is true for the individual believer as well as for the whole Church. Through prayerful contemplation of Sacred Scripture, through unceasing study of God's Word, again and again God speaks anew to us, to his Church. We never come to an end with the Bible. One who becomes involved with it in faith, prayerfully, and with an attentive ear "is like a householder who brings out of his treasure what is new and what is old" (Mt 13:52).

This is beautifully demonstrated particularly by centuries of experience with the psalms, in which "The Word of God becomes man's prayer" (CCC 2587), at all times new and yet familiar from of old. Above all, however, this is evident with the Gospel, in which Christ, the eternal Word of the Father, speaks to us live, in the flesh, lovingly. "It's the Gospels that occupy my mind when I'm at prayer; my poor soul has so many needs, and yet this is the one thing needful" (CCC 127, quoting Saint Thérèse of Lisieux, *Ms. autob.* A 83v).

24

The family—school of prayer

For some years now a monthly magazine has been appearing in France with the simple title *Prier*—To pray! It "specializes" in "helps to prayer": methods, practical instructions for praying, texts of prayers, examples and teachers of prayer, and so on. Its success shows how great a hunger for prayer there is, but also how great a need there is for an introduction to prayer.

The family is often "the first place of education in prayer" (CCC 2685). Table prayers in common, bedtime prayers with parents are the first experience of prayer, which often make a lifelong impression. Two examples for further reflection:

1. I once asked a young nun what the most formative religious experience of her childhood had been. She then recounted how she had burst into her parents' bedroom late one evening without knocking and found them kneeling together beside the bed, praying. When children experience their parents as people of prayer, then prayer does not remain just a childhood routine for them. At the same time they learn that their parents themselves are "children" in God's sight, who not only pray with the children but also speak to God themselves, in their own way. Thus parents will also make proper use of their authority: together with their children they themselves are children of God, who pray confidently to God; for their children they are intercessors who entrust them to God every day.

2. Julian Green, a French-American author, tells of his religious development during childhood. His mother read a lot to him from the Bible, and he liked it very much. One night when he was about five years old, while alone in his room, he had an unforgettable experience of an indescribable presence, which later on he was able to interpret as an experience of God. As a child he did not yet see a direct connection between his usual prayers and this experience. I recall this childhood memory of the novelist whenever the topic turns to the "mystery of God" in the life of a child. As much as parents and family can be the "school of prayer", it still must not be forgotten that God has complete command of "his mystery", which he in his own way can entrust quite personally even to a child. *Everyone Guards His Secret* is the title of a beautiful book by Paul Tournier, a physician from Geneva. Not only should the children sense that their parents have their own prayer life; the parents, too, should think reverently about God's workings in the heart of their child, which are often hidden from them. The story of young Samuel, to whom God speaks at night in the Temple, indicates to us that there can be a message for us grown-ups, too, in children's experience of God's mysterious presence.

A French catechism for children, which has since caught on in many countries (published by the *Institut Notre-Dame de Vie*, F–84210 Venasque), builds upon children's experience of prayer, which is often profound. It is based on the certainty of our faith that the Holy Spirit works in the hearts of children, too, and that they are called to a deep, living contact with God, in the presence of which we adults sometimes can only stand in wonder: "Out of the mouth of infants and of sucklings thou hast perfected praise" (Ps 8:3, Douay-Rheims).

25

Places of prayer

"Every place becomes thy temple, where devotion fills the heart", says the concluding hymn of the *Zweiermesse*, the Schubert Mass. Wherever the heart is lifted up to God is a place of prayer. An experienced urban pastor thinks that nowhere is there so much praying as in the subway. Surely in hospitals there is a lot of prayer. And this was especially true in the trenches during the two World Wars, as many men who experienced and survived them testify. We often hear that one does not need a church in order to pray, that it is better to do so in the woods, in the mountains, in the open country.

"Every place becomes thy temple", and yet it is equally true that we therefore do not make use of all places as a temple or perceive them as a possible area for prayer. Nowadays we run the much greater risk of being kept away from prayer by the noise and distraction in almost every place. Everywhere our senses are "diverted", drawn to something else, so that it has become much more difficult to recollect ourselves, to find some peace and quiet, without which prayer cannot thrive.

"I was glad when they said to me, 'Let us go to the house of the LORD!'" (Ps 122:1). Even the Psalmist experiences the yearning for the place where God is especially near. From time immemorial such a yearning has prompted people to make a pilgrimage, to journey to the house of the Lord, "to see the glory of the Lord".

Because we are beings composed of soul and body, we need places in which God's presence becomes more concentrated. And we need them as a community. That is why we gather together in God's house to worship God; that is also why it is so important to cross the threshold of God's house consciously, so as to make it clear to ourselves that we are in God's presence.

Brother Roger, the prior of the Taizé community, once wrote about the little Romanesque parish church in Taizé: "This place is inhabited." He says this with a view to our Lord present in the Blessed Sacrament. This place of prayer is unparalleled: he himself, truly and mysteriously there, having laid down his life completely for us: "I am the bread of life" (Jn 6:35).

"But when you pray, go into your room" (Mt 6:6). More and more we hear about a "prayer corner", a corner in the house, in one's very own room, where Jesus' word becomes a reality: "Shut the door and pray to your Father who is in secret" (Mt 6:6). Someone who knows how to pray this way in secret will be able to pray "in every place" as well. For him God's temple really will be everywhere, because his heart has become this temple.

26

Prayer and images

Are pictures an aid to prayer or rather a distraction? There can be very different answers to the question: "The beauty of the images moves me to contemplation, as a meadow delights the eyes and subtly infuses the soul with the glory of God", as Saint John Damascene (eighth century) acknowledges,[1] who was one of the great defenders of venerating images during the period of "iconoclasm". The saint lived within the ambit of Islam, which, on the contrary, bans images entirely from the life of prayer, both public and private. The Old Testament prohibition of images (CCC 2129) had only a few exceptions (CCC 2130). The great religions of Asia have various outlooks: whereas strict Buddhism seeks complete detachment from all representations and images, popular Buddhism is exceedingly rich in images, and Hinduism much more so.

Within the realm of Christianity, "iconoclastic" voices (for instance, Calvinism, as well as many "free church" [as opposed to state church] movements) have been heard, again and again, disputing the love in popular piety for images of the saints. What do the great masters of Christian prayer tell us, though?

The "great" Saint Teresa, the reformer of the Car-melite Order and the teacher of "inner prayer" (see

---

[1] *De imag.* 1, 27: PG 94, 1268AB; quoted in CCC 1162.

CCC 2709), gives clear directions on this subject. She was familiar with the view of many spiritual authors that when praying one should strive to leave behind all sense impressions and ascend to the "pure", spiritual contemplation of God, which is devoid of images. Not even Jesus, his face, his life and sufferings, should be the subject of contemplation. To this opinion she made a categorical reply (in chapter 22 of her autobiography): "We are not angels; we have a body!" God himself wants to be near us in a bodily way, and that is why he became man. In the human face of Jesus we encounter God; his life and suffering, his earthly as well as his glorified humanity, are the privileged "place" for our encounter with God. That is why Teresa of Avila emphatically recommends that we look at a picture of the Redeemer as often as possible, so that his image, the sight of him, and thus he himself might be impressed ever more deeply upon our soul, our memory, and our whole life. Her own experience taught her this way: She owed her "second conversion" to a rather fortuitous glance at a statue of the "Man of Sorrows". Deeply moved, she asked Christ to imprint his image indelibly upon her soul. Her prayer was answered. Her experience is shared by the "simple" faithful who realize, in their own way, how much a picture of Christ, of Mary, or of the saints can encourage prayer.

27

Prayer and silence

Mother Teresa of Calcutta (d. 1997) says: "Prayer is difficult if you do not really know how you should pray. To be able to pray, we must learn to be silent. People who can pray are people who love silence."

Peace and quiet have become a precious commodity today. Even in the mountains we are tracked down by noise from the valley or from the airplanes in the sky. The modern world is loud. Where there is a lot of noise, you do not hear well. Hearing loss occurs more and more frequently. In all that noise, conversation founders, too; it is more and more difficult for us to hear each other. So conversation is muted. Spouses, families, suffer from the loss of intimate conversation. The hectic pace of our age, the glittering television screen, the stresses of the working world, the demands of leisure activities—all these things make it more difficult for us to listen to each other and to find words for each other.

This falling silent, however, is not the silence of which Mother Teresa speaks. The silence out of which prayer arises comes from hearing, from attentive listening, from hearkening to the person who speaks to us. "Hear, O Israel", begins God's constant call to his people (Deut 6:4). In order for us to be able to hear God, we must be silent ourselves. Many words are not necessary for prayer, but rather an attentive heart, an "understanding mind"

(1 Kings 3:9). "In praying do not heap up empty phrases as the Gentiles do; for they think that they will be heard for their many words. Do not be like them, for your Father knows what you need before you ask him" (Mt 6:7–8).

How difficult it is to bring the torrent of words to a standstill! When we become quiet externally, usually the internal uproar begins: thoughts pursue one another, everything we think we ought to be doing demands our attention, suddenly seems so urgent. Although we longed for it, silence makes us anxious the moment it stands at the door of the heart and we really have the opportunity to enter into it.

The Dominican mystic John Tauler (fifteenth century) says: "If God is to speak, then things have to be silent. All powers must be silent and prepare a great stillness for God." Sometimes God first has to lead us into the desert in order for us to begin to hear, in order for "things" and "powers" to be silent. "Let go" of yourself, of your worries, of all desires and ideas, fears and memories!

Often our worship services are not much help in attaining this interior peace and quiet, the relinquishing of ourselves for a relationship with the One who awaits us: too many words, too much "action" (as important as this is in the liturgy), too few pauses and moments of quiet! How important it is after Communion to remain at peace, when Christ has come to us in the Blessed Sacrament! Quiet eucharistic adoration is an aid to resting in the Lord with an attentive ear and a loving heart. Ultimately only love can teach us genuine interior silence in God's presence, that "silent love" (CCC 2717, quoting Saint John of the Cross, *Maxims and Counsels*, no. 53)[1] which makes prayer a fruitful encounter with God.

[1] In *The Collected Works of St. John of the Cross*, trans. K. Kavanaugh, O.C.D., and O. Rodriguez, O.C.D. (Washington, D.C.: Institute of Carmelite Studies, 1979), 678.

28

Vocal prayer

Stillness and silence are the soil in which prayer can thrive. Yet if it is to grow, it needs the word. Ever since men have prayed, they have expressed their prayer in words, interior and exterior, with speech and song, but also with gestures, the language of the body.

It is said that prayer is talking with God. That is true, but we would not turn to God in prayer if God had not first spoken to men. Because we are beings composed of body and soul (CCC 1146), God speaks to us in all our senses, and we answer with body and soul.

The Russian priest and theologian Sergei Bulgakov (d. 1940), who in his younger years was an atheist, tells how God spoke to him through an experience of nature and for the first time made him consciously aware of his presence (quoted in M. J. Le Guillou, *Das Geheimnis des Vaters* [Einsiedeln, 1974]): The sight of the Caucasus Mountains, which rise majestically from the Southern Russian plain: "O LORD, our Lord, how majestic is your name in all the earth!" (Ps 8:1).

It is consistent with the bodily-spiritual nature of man that interior prayer should also find a sensible expression (CCC 2702). Saint Dominic, as his confreres observed, especially when he prayed alone at night, used to "embody" his prayer in various bodily postures. Sometimes he would pray prostrate on the floor, then again stretched out toward heaven like an arrow, or else he spread his arms wide in the form of a cross and prayed while bowing profoundly or kneeling. His religious brothers have recorded and interpreted nine such manners of praying. They are real helps to prayer even today.

It is also consistent with the social, gregarious nature of man, however, that we express our prayer in words, that we pray together (CCC 2704). Our liturgical prayer relies upon familiar, well-known prayers; it cannot be "reinvented" each time with complete spontaneity. We need the gestures and rituals of the prayer in which we are at home, into which we can "enter". This becomes especially clear when prayer becomes song. "He who sings, prays twice", so goes a saying attributed to Saint Augustine. Those familiar hymns that go to the heart—how helpful they are for our personal and communal prayer!

Sometimes spontaneous, free prayer is considered to be "more genuine" when compared with formulaic prayer. Fixed prayers supposedly run the risk of becoming the same old story, of being recited mechanically. We are all too familiar with this danger of routine. It is no argument, however, against immersing ourselves in familiar prayers. After all, the Lord himself gave us a prayer that he had formulated, which we will never finish praying: the Our Father. And precisely this prayer, which has been predetermined and entrusted to us, can show us what is ultimately the decisive thing in all vocal prayer, whether spoken or sung: the awareness of him "to whom we speak" (CCC 2704, quoting Saint Teresa of Avila). In his presence external praying becomes an internal action, a prayer of the heart.

29

Meditation leads to prayer

Is meditating already a form of praying, too? "Meditation is above all a quest" (CCC 2705). Meditation means, first of all, reflection about the articles of faith. Therefore to meditate is not yet to pray, but it should lead to prayer. For in pondering what God has to say to us through his Word, through the things in nature and the events in history, prayer can be "enkindled", and meditation can become prayer.

Father Leppich, the great Jesuit preacher and founder of "Action 365", encouraged Christians to make even the daily newspaper an occasion for meditation. This of course demands serious thought about the events in the world, reflection that does not merely take the news as grist for an insatiable curiosity, but rather seeks God's purpose and method in all things. What does God want to say to us through this earthquake, through that war, perhaps through a small, seemingly "insignificant" item among the announcements of the day? The Bible is the great school of meditation: it teaches us not to read the events of history as merely an endless chain of incidents, but rather to recognize God's hand in them and to hear his Word speaking to us through them..

Meditation begins when we go beyond the surface of events, of stories, of texts, and run into traces of the living God; when it is no longer a matter of quenching our thirst for knowledge, of understanding with our reason, but rather of answering the personal question that crops up in meditation: "Lord, what do you want me to do?" (CCC 2706).

So it happened with Saint Ignatius of Loyola, who through his Spiritual Exercises has become for many a teacher of meditation. In the long period of recuperation after his injury in Pamplona, he discovered the method of regular, orderly meditation upon his own life (examination of conscience), but especially upon the life of Christ, so as to see and order his own life in the mirror of Jesus and to make the right decisions according to God's will. The fundamental meditation (Ignatius calls it "principle and foundation") concerns man's final goal, eternal salvation, toward which all thought and actions should be directed. Meditation finds its daily nourishment, preferably, in the Gospel, in the deeds and sufferings of Jesus, in his words and his attitudes.

The goal of meditation is to "internalize" the subject meditated upon, no longer to reflect only upon its exterior, but to taste it from within. What methods to use is a secondary question; they should assist with recollection, with engaging the imagination, with interior and exterior discipline. They can prepare us for the grace that is sought and prayed for in meditation: "that I may know [Christ] and the power of his resurrection" (Phil 3:10).

30

Contemplative prayer—intimacy with God

In the prayer group that I was in during my years in Switzerland, I had a friend with whom I would often talk afterward on the way home from the prayer meeting. He was employed as a gardener. One evening he spoke of something that had been given to him as a priceless treasure: contemplative prayer. He said it was like a spring that had welled up inside of him and flowed constantly from then on. "It prays within me", is how he described this stream of interior union with God.

Is that an "exceptional state" that is granted to only a few people who have been very specially graced? What is this contemplative prayer, which according to the unanimous testimony of the Christian masters is the genuine, true prayer, that worship "in spirit and in truth" of which Jesus speaks to the woman at Jacob's well and about which he says, "thus the Father seeks to be worshipped" (cf. Jn 4:23–24)? It is not an outstanding performance by the elite in the field of spirituality, but rather it is that interior intimacy with God which is intended for all baptized people, to which Jesus wants to lead all his disciples, because it is his own intimacy with the Father.

Saint Teresa of Avila understands contemplative prayer as friendship with God, taking time frequently to be alone with the heart's Beloved (CCC 2709). No sooner have we said that, than our heart knows what is meant—

at least in yearning for it. We know how this intimacy "tastes"; we know also, though, how much it must be sought, striven, and prayed for and that it is ultimately granted as a gift (CCC 2710).

Like every friendship, this one also needs its special times, in which everything else is set aside and our only reason for being there is to "contemplate" the other: "I look at him and he looks at me," said a peasant to the Curé of Ars, who often saw him spending time in front of the tabernacle (CCC 2715). Given times of silent listening, of lovingly being in his presence, contemplative prayer can then become something like a "permanent state", which extends even into sleep as a watchfulness of the heart.

Thus Jesus' prayer to the Father was probably a never-ending dialogue. There is no doubt that Jesus wants to bring us all into his prayer (CCC 2718). That requires, not any special mastery, but rather simply being "child-like" before God: we may be certain that there are many "little ones", simple and humble souls who—without knowing it and without being able to put a name to their experience—live this deep prayer of intimacy with God.

Jesus, of course, can bestow it upon us only if we "watch and pray" with him in his hours of darkness and in our own (Mt 26:40; CCC 2719). Then contemplative prayer acquires a "missionary" character; it then desires to be consumed, like Jesus himself, in dedication to others: the friend lays down his life (Jn 15:13)!

The battle of prayer

Anyone who tries to follow the path of prayer inevitably discovers that prayer is a battle, indeed, a difficult battle. If we pray only when we want to, when we feel like it, we will not pray much; in fact, we will grow unaccustomed to prayer. To be sure, prayer is a grace, but it is still our answer, which we can either give God or refuse him, which we must intend and for which we ought to fight. The battle to pray is part of the battle demanded by the Christian life as a whole. We will pray as we live and live as we pray (CCC 2725).

As we look at several aspects of this battle in the following pages, it should be clear from the outset that we can engage in this battle joyfully and full of confidence, because we know in faith that our Father in heaven knows how weak we are and how much we need his help. Saint Paul encourages us: "Likewise the Spirit helps us in our weakness; for we do not know how to pray as we ought, but the Spirit himself intercedes for us with sighs too deep for words. . . . [T]he Spirit intercedes for the saints according to the will of God" (Rom 8:26–27).

We are not alone in the battle of prayer; just as a mother teaches her child to speak, so, too, the Lord teaches us through his Spirit. Heaven is sure to help; angels and saints assist us. And yet we cannot avoid fighting the battle ourselves.

The first battlefield is our time. We have to battle constantly with the temptation to believe that we have no time. A day has to accommodate so much, and it is so easy to sacrifice prayer first for the sake of everything else. Then when we look back over the day, very often we must admit: the time that we withheld from prayer is the time we then squandered needlessly on something else. Conversely, experience teaches that time devoted to prayer is not deducted from something else; it is given back in "good measure".

Often, though, we have to battle with an even greater obstacle: There is "nothing to be gained" from prayer, or so the "spirit of the age" tries to convince us. Perhaps we do realize that meditation helps us to quiet down and recollect ourselves. But prayer? God seems so distant, and if it is true that prayer is speaking with God, then it looks as if the one is speaking while the other remains silent. To put the challenge even more radically: What is prayer supposed to accomplish anyway? Can it change the course of events? Or will God still be not only mute but also indifferent? Because we have doubts about prayer, have so little faith in its efficacy, we immediately become discouraged by the battle to make time for prayer. The battle for prayer thus proves to be a battle for faith: in faith, people in need turned to Jesus. Let us follow their example!

Distractions

Who has not been troubled by distractions while praying? We rarely, perhaps never, succeed in saying one Our Father with undivided attention, without letting our thoughts wander, without suddenly being somewhere else mentally. Again and again I hear the complaint of older people: "It is so hard for me to concentrate"; their attention remains focused for only a short time. Is the situation any better for the priest who celebrates Holy Mass? How often we discover, in the most sacred moments, that something entirely different from the action of the Mass is going through our heads. Anyone who had the opportunity to observe Padre Pio will remember one thing above all else: here was someone who celebrated Mass in such a manner that he was completely involved in, in no way distracted from, what is accomplished on the altar—Christ, who sacrifices himself for us, Body and Blood, and gives himself to us.

What was the secret of this recollection? How can we fight our distractions? "If you have never suffered from distractions, then you do not know how to pray", says the Trappist monk Thomas Merton. Let us not be alarmed, then, by distractions; they can become a salutary way of prayer. As long as prayer is an easy, joyful, almost offhanded activity, we are likely to believe that we have already made great progress. Distractions make us more sober in several respects, and that can help us to go farther along the way of prayer.

When we become quiet in prayer, when the mud stirred up in the water has settled, we begin to see many things within us more clearly than the hectic everyday routine allows. Many a thing then comes to light that we prefer to overlook. First we discover, in that quiet, in prayer, that suddenly all sorts of things appear to be very important and urgent and have to be taken care of immediately, so that we are just about ready to run away from prayer. The only remedy against this distraction is the struggle simply to remain there and keep praying as long as we had resolved to at the start. Spiritual masters recommend quitting prayer not one minute sooner than we intended (unless a real obligation of charity to our neighbor calls us).

When we persevere in prayer, we are often besieged by multitudes of thoughts, fantasies, ideas that are difficult for us to control, that force their way out of all the cracks of our subconscious and our memory into our consciousness once it is calmed down. We can try to drive them away, as the cow swats flies with her tail: they come back! It is better to look to God and to bring to him our need in the midst of distractions: "See, Lord, how little I can keep my heart in your presence!" Yet the longing to do so is already a victory over the bothersome swarm.

The most difficult distractions to combat are those that come from our duties, our work, our pressing concerns. They painfully reveal to us the limitations on our ability to place everything in God's hand, so as to remain thus with complete confidence in his presence.

To acknowledge this humbly will awaken our love for him who says to us: "Give me everything, including your worries and even your distractions!"

33

Aridity

It, too, is part of the experience of prayer: no feelings, no enthusiasm, no exalted or profound thoughts. Desert. Dry spell. Persevering through the drought becomes a test of fidelity, of determination. On their way to the Promised Land, the people of God became thoroughly acquainted with the desert; forty years God tested them, freed them from their old attachments to Egypt, in order to make them his People.

Included in the desert experience are the grumbling and complaining, the looking back to the "fleshpots" of Egypt (Num 11:4–6), and also the bitter experiences of feuding and rebellion, of recourse to the false gods, of falling away from the true God.

Christian tradition has always read the story about the wandering of Israel in the desert as an archetype also for the soul's journey with God. When God decides to draw us to himself, that often happens at first through experiences of intense joy, of interior consolation and ardent feelings. Prayer is a delight, and the emotions are not shortchanged. Soon, though, the person praying goes through the first desert experiences. The separation from "Egypt", from old habits, from old familiar pleasures, starts to be painful. The joy of praying is no longer attractive; prayer is perceived as dry and barren; all sorts of other things demand priority and seem more important than prayer time. The worrisome question arises of whether God has withdrawn, whether we have distanced ourselves from him. Why this reluctance in the soul, this lack of feeling and absence of joy?

The "desert experience" of the individual resembles that of the People of God. The first thing to remember is that God is leading us through it. And he does it out of love for us: he wants to free us from our former slavery, from the fetters of our own making to which we have grown accustomed, even though we suffer from them. The "desert" is supposed to make us free, and that is why God allows us to experience times of dryness. When God apparently withdraws, we begin to seek him. So he leads us, in prayer, to seek, not ourselves, but him, to cling, not to our experiences and feelings, but to him.

Dryness has another effect, too: it shows us our neediness and poverty. As long as prayer is full of delight, we can imagine that we are already quite perfect. The desert makes us recognize that Jesus' saying applies to us: "Apart from me you can do nothing" (Jn 15:5; cf. CCC 2732).

Aridity can also make us terribly aware that the ground of our life has become hard and has dried up, because our everyday cares and worries, our lack of fidelity to prayer, and the dulling of our heart have taken us far from God. Then "the battle requires conversion [cf. Lk 8:6, 13]" (CCC 2731). And God, who is close to the contrite heart, will grant anew the joy of experiencing his nearness.

34

Trust

"Filial trust is tested—it proves itself—in tribulation [cf. Rom 5:3–5]" (CCC 2734). When prayer becomes a battle, when distractions, dryness, challenges of every kind beset us and try to keep us from prayer, threaten to discourage us, that is the hour of trust. Trust is victorious over all temptations to give up and leave off praying.

These temptations can take various forms: the temptation to give priority to everything else but prayer, because so many things are pressing and appear to be more important. If prayer is then neglected more and more, an aversion to it can set in, which the old spiritual masters called *acedia* (CCC 2733), a "spiritual apathy", which has effects like those of a depression but is rooted in spiritual rather than physical or mental causes. Acedia can be the result of spiritual carelessness or improper or immoral conduct. Its deepest roots are pride and presumption, which usually go hand in hand with despondency. "I know", says the Little Flower, "that discouragement is also a form of pride." "The humble are not surprised by their distress; it leads them to trust more, to hold fast in constancy" (CCC 2733).

Saint Thérèse of Lisieux writes to her sister Céline: "I am not always faithful, but I never become discouraged." Because she did not allow herself to become discouraged by her weaknesses and failings, she inspires so many people with the courage to trust and simply to let themselves "fall into Jesus' arms", as she was fond of saying.

Given this attitude, she can at any time make living contact with Jesus in prayer: "O Jesus, how happy I would be if I had been completely faithful. But unfortunately, I am often sad in the evening, because I feel that I could have responded better to Your grace. . . . If I were more united with You, more loving toward my sisters, humbler and more selfless, it would be less difficult to speak with You in prayer. And yet, my God, far from being discouraged at the sight of my miseries, I come to You full of confidence, for I remember that 'Those who are well have no need of a physician, but those who are sick'" (Prayer no. 7).

This trust, as Thérèse repeats again and again, knows no limits. Because it entrusts itself to God completely, it is full of confidence even in the midst of all sorts of afflictions. Yet it is always in need of nourishment, like a fire that must be stoked. It is the little acts of love that feed the fire. They constantly renew our awareness that our trusting, our praying, our loving is always nothing more than a new response to an incomprehensible love that comes to meet us.

35

Is our prayer heard?

In a little pilgrimage church in Switzerland, they say, there is a votive offering on which is written: "Thank you, Mary, for not hearing my prayer." We do not always see as clearly as this petitioner that it is a good thing when God does not grant all our requests. Sometimes we recognize very clearly that God's will and his loving providence are manifested quite differently from the way that we would like. Yet it can also cause a serious crisis of faith if a prayer offered in great distress is not answered, if, for example, a child storms heaven asking God for the healing of his cancer-stricken mother, but without success. In such situations, what are we supposed to make of words like these: "Ask, and it will be given you. . . . For every one who asks receives" (Lk 11:9–10)? Did the child spend too little time in prayer? Did God take no notice of his tears? After all, one cannot say about him what Saint James severely charges the adults with: "You do not have, because you do not ask. You ask and do not receive, because you ask wrongly, to spend it on your passions" (Jas 4:2–3).

There is, of course, such a thing as the request of a divided heart that has not been purified, that must first go through the cleansing fire. We can ask for everything, but Jesus teaches us to ask first for the one thing necessary: that his will be done, as it is in heaven, so too in our lives. The Lord gave us an example of this in his own life, when he implored his Father, out of the depths of his fear, praying that "this cup" might pass from him: "Nevertheless, not as I will, but as you will" (Mt 26:39).

Can we say, then, that God hears every prayer, "but not as we will, but rather as he wills it"? But do we know what he wills and what we should ask for in the right way? What better way, though, of coming to know his will than to lay all our desires before him openly? Naturally God knows what is in our hearts much better than we do ourselves. Yet by telling him all our longings and hopes, fears and requests, we bring them, so to speak, into his light. In this light we begin to see more clearly what there is about our requests that is lasting in his sight. The more open our hearts become toward him, the more we will bring before him even the smallest things in childlike trust, and the more confident we will be to ask for great things, the greatest things, just as little Saint Thérèse with complete confidence prayed for the eternal salvation of the serial killer Pranzini: her heart had learned to pray for the right thing, the most important thing: that no one be lost! "Transformation of the praying heart is the first response [of God] to our petition" (CCC 2739).

36

"Pray constantly"

How can we respond to this challenge of the Apostle Paul (1 Thess 5:17)? It is obviously not a pious exaggeration, but simply repeats what Jesus said to those who listened to him: "that they ought always to pray and not lose heart" (Lk 18:1).

How can we pray at all times? From the earliest days this question has occupied the spiritual masters of Christendom. Yet before we deal with the question "How", we must ask about "Why". Why pray, and why pray "constantly"?

Because prayer is as essential as breathing and a heartbeat. In the *Catechism* there is a startling saying of a great saint, who was an extremely kind and loving man: "Those who pray are certainly saved; those who do not pray are certainly damned", says Alphonsus Liguori, the founder of the Redemptorists (CCC 2744, quoting *Del gran mezzo della preghiera*). If praying means relating to God, then it is clear that the man without this relationship cannot live, since in him we live and move and have our being (Acts 17:28). Just as a man without human relationships perishes spiritually and even physically, so it happens also to the man with no relationship to God. Prayer is the life, the breath of the soul, the heartbeat of the true life.

But how should this be done, practically speaking? Starting out from Jesus' command to pray without ceasing, the Eastern Church developed the practice of the "Jesus Prayer", which in recent times has become familiar to many people in our part of the world, too, especially through *The Way of a Pilgrim*. The spiritual master (*staretz*) who shows the pilgrim the way says to him: "The ceaseless interior Jesus Prayer is the uninterrupted . . . invocation of the divine Name of Jesus Christ with the lips, with the mind, and with the heart, whereby one calls to mind his constant presence and asks him for his mercy, during any activity, anywhere, at any time, even while sleeping." The Jesus Prayer can be as follows: "Lord Jesus Christ, have mercy on me", or even simply "Jesus!" The pilgrim speaks of the great consolation that he experienced in this way, and of how the prayer gradually "flowed out from him entirely by itself".

Yet it would be a misunderstanding to see the Jesus Prayer primarily as a technique, a method of prayer. It is rather an "affair of the heart", which is familiar to Jewish believers as well: always being mindful of God, not forgetting him who never forgets us. "Standing before God [= remaining in his presence]" is the foundation of prayer, "with the heart and forevermore, day and night . . . until the end of your life", says the Orthodox saint Bishop Theophane (1815–1894).

We can always do that, though, while working as well as during formal prayer. "We are destined to be united with God during work time through our work and to be united with him during prayer time through our prayer", says the simple Carmelite Brother Lawrence (1611–1691).

The basis for this union with God, which is always possible, is not our doing, but rather his pledge: "I am with you always" (Mt 28:20). Even though we often respond imperfectly, there is still one response that we can make constantly: the longing of our hearts!

37

The Lord's Prayer

"We do not know how to pray as we ought." Thus Saint Paul sums up an experience that is common to many people. That is why "the Spirit helps us in our weakness"; he "intercedes for us with sighs too deep for words. . . . [T]he Spirit intercedes for the saints according to the will of God" (Rom 8:26–27).

How do we learn to pray "according to the will of God"? By learning to pray as Jesus did: "[Jesus] was praying in a certain place, and when he ceased, one of his disciples said to him, 'Lord, teach us to pray'" (Lk 11:1). And as a result Jesus gave his disciples the Our Father. But what does the Lord teach by means of this prayer? What does the Our Father tell us about how Jesus prayed and how the Holy Spirit teaches us to pray correctly?

Many great Christian masters have written commentaries on the Our Father. The *Catechism of the Catholic Church* summarizes much of what has been accumulated in Christianity's long experience of prayer (CCC 2759–2865). In the following short chapters we do not intend to summarize the *Catechism* yet again, but rather to listen carefully, with its help, to what the Holy Spirit wants to say to us "with sighs too deep for words" (Rom 8:26) through the words of this prayer.

The Evangelist Matthew records the Our Father in the middle of the Sermon on the Mount (Mt 5:1—

7:29). In the Beatitudes (Mt 5:3–11) and in the instructions of the Sermon on the Mount, Jesus proclaims the way of life that corresponds completely to the will of God—the only one, therefore, that can make us happy and blessed; he teaches us the same thing in the Our Father in the form of seven petitions (Mt 6:9–13). By means of them we should ask the Father for things that contribute to salvation, happiness, and prosperity.

Happy will be the one who lives as a child of God. The Sermon on the Mount is the school of divine adoption, of living in the spirit of sonship (Gal 4:5), by "the Spirit of his Son", who cries out in our hearts, "Abba! Father!" (Gal 4:6). How do we become, though, what we already are (through baptism): God's children, people who are so familiar with God that they can really call him "Father", as Jesus did?

The seven petitions of the Lord's Prayer (CCC 2765) contain not only *what* we are to ask for as we ought, but also *how* we should ask for these things, in what sequence and order. It teaches us to set the right priorities in our lives, as God orders things. When this prayer makes more and more of an impression upon us and orients our lives, then we are being "formed" according to the image and example of Jesus; we become new men, truly "perfect, as your heavenly Father is perfect" (Mt 5:48).

38

Father

The first word of the Lord's Prayer is also its essential subject. All the petitions follow from the fact that, thanks to Jesus' instruction, we are allowed to address God as FATHER. The shorter version of the prayer, which Saint Luke records, begins: "Father, hallowed be your name" (Lk 11:2).

What does this mean, to refer to God as Father? Is it the heritage of the "patriarchal" world view of that time, which gave precedence everywhere to men over women? Many people think that this should be corrected and improved today, that God should be addressed as Father and Mother. That must be opposed resolutely. Jesus did not adopt the notions of his day, but rather revealed to us the mystery of God, which no era, no people, no culture, no philosophy or religion could ever know or imagine on its own.

"Tam pater, nemo", says Tertullian (third century) with the unsurpassable conciseness of the Latin language: So much a father as he, no one else is. "No one is father as God is Father" (CCC 239).

Human fatherhood (and motherhood) is the image of God's Fathering, though they will never attain the fullness of the archetype. But in Jesus' preaching, and even more in his life, it becomes evident what a great gift is bestowed upon us, that we are permitted to call God "Father". It must have been quite extraordinary to hear

Jesus speak about his Father, and even more so to hear Him speak *to* Him as "Abba"—"dear Papa". No one has ever seen God; only the One who rests upon the Father's bosom has made him known (cf. John 1:18).

But have not other religions referred to God as Father, too? Did not the Old Testament, at least, do that? Certainly there is a general religious sense that God, being the origin of everything, is in a certain way the Father of mankind and of the universe. The Jewish faith, too, is acquainted with this form of address, since it calls God the Father of Israel (cf. especially Hos 11:1ff.; Is 63:15ff.). Yet the way Jesus reveals himself as "the Son" and bears witness to God as his Father is something new. So new that it encountered vehement opposition.

When Jesus teaches his disciples to pray to the "Father", this means a new being for them, a new reality. The handing on of the Our Father is an important milestone along the path to adult baptism. As the prayer of the members of the Body of Christ, it is a preparation for receiving of the Body of Christ in the celebration of the Eucharist. It is the prayer of those who have been reborn in water and in the Holy Spirit. Those who have received the Spirit of Jesus, the Spirit of "sonship" or of "divine adoption", can therefore cry out with complete confidence: "Abba, Father!" (Rom 8:15; Gal 4:6). We can spend an entire lifetime discovering what a wonderful thing it is that he is our "Abba, Father".

39

Our Father

"Call no man your father on earth, for you have one Father, who is in heaven" (Mt 23:9). "You are all brethren" (Mt 23:8). The fact that Jesus commands us to address God as "our Father" also means that we are children of one Father, that we should become and be such children. "Love your enemies and pray for those who persecute you, so that you may be sons of your Father who is in heaven; for he makes his sun rise on the evil and on the good, and sends rain on the just and on the unjust" (Mt 5:44–45).

What does it mean to be allowed to address God as our Father? Has this prayer become "an expression of piety for all people" (Romano Guardini), the token of a common fraternity of all men? Too rarely do we remark, as the old introduction to the Lord's Prayer does, what an audacious thing it is to address God as Father ("we dare to say", cf. CCC 2777). When Jesus repeatedly spoke about or to God as his Father, this had extremely serious consequences: "This was why the Jews sought all the more to kill him, because he . . . called God his Father, making himself equal with God" (Jn 5:18).

Does Jesus make his disciples equal with himself, if they now can call God their Father, too? He, the eternal Son of God, who became man, can express as man his eternal relationship to the Father: he, as no one else, can say "Father"; we may say it, because "God has sent the

Spirit of his Son into our hearts, crying, 'Abba! Father'!"
(Gal 4:6). We are allowed to call God Father because
Christ has obtained for us the "adoption as sons" (Gal
4:5).

Who is included, then, in the "Our"? First, of course,
the baptized, which is why the Our Father is also the
ecumenical prayer (CCC 2791). For this reason the Our
Father is also "handed over" or entrusted to the newly
baptized: in and through Christ they are now accepted
in the Son as sons by grace: "[The adjective] 'Our'
Father . . . , as used by us, does not express possession,
but an entirely new relationship with God" (CCC 2786).
And this relationship is granted to us in baptism, which
is what really allows us to call God our Father.

Are the "others" excluded on that account? Is God
not the Father of all mankind? "God's love has no
bounds, neither should our prayer" (CCC 2793). Precisely because the Our Father is the prayer of those who
have become, with Jesus, sons and daughters of the one
Father, this prayer should be as far-reaching as the love
of the Father, who wants "all men to be saved and to
come to the knowledge of the truth" (1 Tim 2:4). The
deeper this prayer leads us into Jesus' prayer, the wider
becomes the circle of those for whom we pray it as Jesus
intends. It opens us to the full scope of Jesus' mission,
which the Father gives him.

40

Our Father who art in heaven

Jesus frequently speaks of his "Father in heaven": "Let your light so shine before men, that they may see your good works and give glory to your Father who is in heaven" (Mt 5:16). "Love your enemies and pray for those who persecute you, so that you may be sons of your Father who is in heaven; for he makes his sun rise on the evil and on the good" (Mt 5:44–45). "For if you forgive men their trespasses, your heavenly Father also will forgive you" (Mt 6:14). And, summarizing everything: "You, therefore, must be perfect, as your heavenly Father is perfect" (Mt 5:48).

"Heaven"—this word makes us think, first, of "up there", of things that are high above the earth, the "firmament". Now we know, of course, that God does not "dwell in heaven" in this sense, as perhaps we imagined it as children. And yet it was not simply false, the childish things that were said about the heavenly Father who lives "above the starry canopy". For the place "up there", above the "star-studded heavens"—even if it does lead us into the unimaginable depths and distances of outer space—is still a symbol for the fact that our "here below" is not everything, that we are pilgrims here, making our way to a higher realm that we seek, that we watch for, and that we figuratively call "heaven" as well.

Often while praying, man spontaneously looks up to heaven. During the celebration of the Eucharist, the priest imitates Jesus: "taking the five loaves and the two fish he looked up to heaven, and blessed . . ." (Mt 14:19).

"Our Father, who art in heaven"—that is first of all an indication that our home is in heaven, because we are at home where our Father is. That is where our hearts should be if that place really is our treasure (cf. Mt 6:21): "If then you have been raised with Christ, seek the things that are above, where Christ is, seated at the right hand of God" (Col 3:1).

Yet the reverse is also true: wherever the Father is, heaven is there, and where the will of the Father is done, heaven comes down to earth: "If a man loves me, he will keep my word, and my Father will love him, and we will come to him and make our home with him" (Jn 14:23).

If the first impulse of prayer is a longing for that place up there, for the heavenly homeland, it is at the same time joined with the petition that there might be a heaven on earth, that heaven might "come down to us". This is precisely what all seven petitions of the Lord's Prayer ask for: that heaven might no longer be so far away, that God our Father may be in our hearts and in our lives, not only in heaven someday, up there, but also here and now on earth.

And to the extent that we become children of God, a bit of heaven is already realized on earth. Blessed Elizabeth of the Trinity prays in this way in her well-known prayer, "O My God, Trinity": "Grant my soul peace. Make it your heaven, your beloved dwelling and the place of your rest" (CCC 260). Saint Augustine, too: "[The phrase] 'Our Father, who art in heaven' is rightly understood to mean that God is in the hearts of the just, as in his holy temple. At the same time, it means that those who pray should desire the one they invoke to dwell in them" (CCC 2794, quoting *De serm. Dom. in monte* 2, 5, 18: PL 34, 1277).

41

Hallowed be thy name

The first of the seven petitions is a wish. It expresses the heartfelt desire of Jesus, his inmost concern, the thing to which he devotes his entire life and death: "Father, glorify your name" (Jn 12:28). "We could paraphrase Jesus' prayer intention as follows: 'Father, may you be glorified, may your glory be made visible'" (H. Schürmann).

"At the beginning of the prayer, according to Jesus' instruction, the disciple should first simply proclaim his fondest wish, his most urgent concern: May God's greatness and glory and divinity be recognized and manifested" (H. Schürmann).

Saint Ignatius of Loyola made this wish his motto: "To the greater glory of God". In the life of Jesus, this petition takes a central place: no other wish, no desire moves the heart of Jesus more than the glorification of the Father.

Now this desire—which, as such, is all too often foreign to us self-centered men, because we seek glory from one another and not the glory that comes from God (Jn 5:44)—is furthermore clothed in a language that is even more foreign to us: "Hallowed be thy name." What does this wish for "hallowing" mean, and what is meant by "name"?

"'Name' means more than a mere designation: It contains the essence of the thing named. The name is something mysterious; it stands for the one himself who bears the name" (Romano Guardini). The first, most intimate desire that Jesus urges upon us is that God's name, and thus God himself, be "hallowed"; that means, that he might be magnified, "made great", and be manifested as holy. This desire animates Jesus' whole life and his every deed.

Now, though, the prayer asks that his name "be" hallowed. This passive form is a paraphrase of the very name of God: may God himself manifest his name as holy, may he make his glory and holiness visible. The person praying expects God's victory in the events of history, the shining forth of his holiness, the coming of his kingdom (as the second petition specifies).

Yet the "hallowing of his name" has a very concrete meaning, for which we pray in the Our Father: Jesus himself is the "Holy One of God", the One in whom God's name has appeared among us and has dwelt among us. When Jesus prays, "Father, glorify your name," the voice from heaven answers: "I have glorified it, and I will glorify it again" (Jn 12:28).

Now when we, too, pray that the Father may hallow his name through us, that we may keep his name holy, this is first of all the petition that we may be worthy of Jesus, that we may do honor to Christ's name through our lives (CCC 2814). That we may not, through a contrary life, "blaspheme that honorable name" of Jesus "by which [we] are called" in baptism (Jas 2:7). We have complete confidence in the Father, that he will grant this in answer to Jesus' petition, who was glorified, hallowed for us, so that we, too, might truly be hallowed (cf. Jn 17:7–10).

42

Thy kingdom come

"The second petition of the Our Father leads us into the innermost thoughts of Jesus' heart" (Romano Guardini). It makes concrete the first great prayer petition, that the name of our Father in heaven be hallowed: May he establish his dominion, may his sovereign rule commence and his kingdom come visibly, mightily, and definitively!

What do we pray for in this fervent petition? What does it mean for Jesus; what should it mean for us? In the Sermon on the Mount, Jesus says it clearly: "Seek first his kingdom and his righteousness, and all these things shall be yours as well" (Mt 6:33). The kingdom of God is first and foremost in Jesus' preaching: "The time is fulfilled, and the kingdom of God is at hand; repent, and believe in the gospel" (Mk 1:15). "Nowhere does Jesus define precisely and exhaustively what he understands by the kingdom of God" (H. Schürmann). Yet he speaks of it in many parables, and it is always "his central proclamation. . . . The coming of God's kingdom is the sum and substance of Jesus' preaching" (H. Schürmann).

As with all the petitions of the Lord's Prayer, we must hear the first word along with it: "Father, . . . thy kingdom come." Only this intimately familiar "Abba" of Jesus gives the petition its full urgency: May thy rule, thy kingship finally come, be made manifest, and go into effect! For only from the Father's kingdom can we, without falling into utopian illusions, expect real freedom, justice, and victory over sin and death.

Have we not waited too long already for the promised kingdom that we implore? If we expect the complete fulfillment of this petition in this life, we deceive ourselves. The kingdom of God and of Christ "is not of this world" (Jn 18:36). No social or cultural arrangement, no political or even religious institution on earth will ever be the kingdom of God. The Church has always rejected such utopian expectations ("millenarianism") (CCC 676). Rather, this petition reaches longingly for the definitive kingdom of God in the next life. Concretely, we look forward to this coming as Christ's Second Coming at the end of time (CCC 2817).

"Far from distracting the Church from her mission in this present world, this desire commits her to it all the more strongly" (CCC 2818). By yearning with Jesus for the kingdom of his Father, and placing it first and foremost, it is already realized in the world, like a "seed" within us. Of course this coming, which is ultimately the coming of Jesus' dominion, meets with resistance and rejection. Jesus proclaimed the kingdom of God, but what came was the dominion of the adversary, the "ruler of this world" (Jn 12:31). "The hour of darkness came, and it was as though the kingdom retreated" (R. Guardini). Because we were unwilling (cf. Lk 13:34), God's dominion comes through Jesus' Cross: in our place he realizes the one and only thing that can establish the kingdom of God on earth: complete submission to God's will, so that he alone can decide everything.

Thus the petition: "Father, . . . thy kingdom come", is the urgent plea that everything opposed to his dominion—everything, therefore, that keeps people, history, and the world in bondage—might be overcome through Jesus, through his victory on the Cross. And it is the request that we might see even now the signs of this victory, wherever God's will goes into effect.

43

Thy will be done, on earth as it is in heaven

"It is an intolerable situation that God's holy 'will' is not done on earth" (H. Schürmann). There is no happiness without conformity to the will of God. Where his will is not done, there is unhappiness and trouble. The petition that the Father's will be done is inspired by a great yearning, an intense longing for all to be well, by the painful awareness that so many things "on earth" are not well. As in the first two petitions, the basic idea here in the third is the certainty that there is nothing we need more urgently, nothing better that can happen, than that his will be done. Do we sense Jesus' most fervent longing in these petitions?

What is the will of the Father, though? Paul professes it in these terms: "He has made known to us . . . the mystery of his will, according to his purpose which he set forth in Christ as a plan for the fulness of time, to unite all things in him, things in heaven and things on earth. In him, according to the purpose of him who accomplishes all things according to the counsel of his will, we who first hoped in Christ have been destined and appointed to live for the praise of his glory" (Eph 1:9–11). "We ask insistently for this loving plan to be fully realized on earth as it is already in heaven" (CCC 2823). And this petition is none other than that his kingdom come, that his name be hallowed.

The decree of his will is for "all men to be saved" (1 Tim 2:4). For this purpose the Father sent the Son into the world; for this purpose Jesus came, "to do your will, O God" (Heb 10:7). Because Christ, as man, fulfilled the will of the Father wholly and absolutely, the kingdom of God comes to us through him, and through him alone. By laying down his life for us, for all of mankind, Jesus "hallowed" or glorified the Father's name.

Now we, too, should pray the Father that what Jesus has fulfilled might be realized everywhere "on earth" in us, in all men. Jesus, in teaching us to ask for this, also shows us that we cannot fulfill the will of the Father by our own unaided power. There is too much resistance within us: self-will, which we can certainly fight against but cannot overcome by ourselves.

"Not my will, but yours be done" (Lk 22:42). If Jesus, who was entirely sinless, prayed in this way on the Mount of Olives, how much more do we need to make this petition, in order to overcome the resistance to God's will that is caused by sin.

Probably another aspect of this petition is too often overlooked: wherever men on earth do the will of the Father, the family of Jesus grows; there the Church's inmost meaning is realized: "Whoever does the will of God is my brother, and sister, and mother" (Mk 3:35). In the middle of this family of Jesus stands Mary, who shows us how we can become Jesus' brothers and sisters and helps us to behave accordingly.

44

Give us this day our daily bread

After the three "you-petitions" come the four "us-petitions". The first three direct our hearts to Jesus' primary concern, to his most fervent and heartfelt prayer: "Father, glorify your Name" (Jn 12:28). God does this by making his kingdom come and by accomplishing his will. In the four "us-petitions", we should now ask our Father in heaven for the things that accomplish his will on earth, too.

Since he is the Father of us all, we should ask him first for "our daily bread". This petition is entirely in line with the trust to which Jesus exhorts us in the Sermon on the Mount: "Do not be anxious about your life, what you shall eat. . . . [Y]our heavenly Father knows that you need them all" (Mt 6:25, 32).

As well as bread, we should ask for the forgiveness of our trespasses, preservation from temptation, and deliverance from evil. These petitions indicate, first of all, great tribulations: "Someone who is in dire need does not furnish long explanations; instead, he shouts for help" (H. Schürmann).

The four petitions are actually cries in distress. Only in light of the first three petitions, though, can we begin to realize the depth of this distress: Does not spiritual experience teach us that the world's needs can be seen properly only in light of God's kingdom and his righteousness (cf. Mt 6:33)? How profound the pangs of human guilt and sin, how oppressing the temptations, how enslaving the power of evil, how tormenting the hunger for material and spiritual bread—this becomes apparent for the first time to the one upon whom shines the hope of the coming kingdom of God. Accordingly, the prayer is offered that much more forcefully to the One who alone can satisfy the hunger, forgive the trespasses, and deliver from evil.

In all simplicity we are to ask for bread, the quintessential nourishment. Certainly, this does not exempt us from the effort involved in working for our daily sustenance: "In the sweat of your face you shall eat bread" (Gen 3:19). And yet, despite all the necessary effort, "everything depends on God's blessing."

But for what sort of bread should we both work and at the same time ask? "Do not labor for the food which perishes, but for the food which endures to eternal life" (Jn 6:27). The daily bread that he gives is not only nourishment for the body; it is "the bread of love", which we live on, without which we perish. It is "the bread of life" (Jn 6:48), which is Jesus himself, who gives himself to us as food.

The "daily bread"—in Greek this is a puzzling word that can be found only here (CCC 2837). It can mean "the bread for tomorrow"—enough for just one day, and he will provide for the subsequent days just as he does for tomorrow, for today. To discover his provident care for us in the present day, to trust in it—that is what this petition teaches us, for he is our Father!

45

And forgive us our trespasses
as we forgive those who trespass against us

The original text speaks of "debts", and they are gigantic, unpayable. Jesus repeatedly and quite clearly states what the matter is: Our "debts" to God are infinitely great. Debts result when you do not pay what you owe. Our indebtedness toward God is enormous, "because we always fall short of God's demands" (H. Schürmann).

In the Sermon on the Mount, Jesus makes us realize that we become indebted to God not only through the "big" sins: "You shall not kill, commit adultery, bear false witness. . . ." We incur debts even through the wicked thoughts of the heart, the lustful look, insincerity of heart, but above all through our omissions: "As you did it not to one of the least of these, you did it not to me" (Mt 25:45).

Through his Spirit, which has been poured into our hearts (cf. Rom 5:5), Christ has revealed to us and made us see how much we resist and evade God's will, even in the innermost recesses of our soul, how often we seek and prefer self, in short: how far removed we are from loving God "with all our heart, with all our soul, with all our mind" (cf. Mt 22:37), and how little we love our neighbor as ourselves (Mt 22:39).

Jesus includes all mankind in the "we" of this petition, for none of us can exempt himself from the common possession of "our debts" and place himself above the others. Our Lord underscores how urgent this insight is by commenting himself on this petition, the only one that he elaborates: "For if you forgive men their trespasses, your heavenly Father also will forgive you; but if you do not forgive men their trespasses, neither will your Father forgive your trespasses" (Mt 6:14–15).

Yet this is precisely what our Father wants to do for us, and if we are supposed to pray that his will be done and his kingdom come, then we also pray that his will may transform our hearts, so that we can forgive each other "from the heart" (cf. Mt 18:35); for if we do not do this, neither can our hard hearts receive God's mercy, which in Christ we can draw upon in limitless quantity.

The way the fifth petition is phrased assumes that we have already forgiven: "as we forgive those who trespass against us". Since we know how rarely we have already done that "from the heart", it is not so much a question here of stating something that has been accomplished as it is of making an additional request to our Father, that he might grant us the grace of being able to forgive, even our enemies (Mt 5:43–44). Only then will we really be children of our Father in heaven.

46

And lead us not into temptation

"Let no one say when he is tempted, 'I am tempted by God'; for God cannot be tempted with evil and he himself tempts no one" (Jas 1:13).

Is James, the brother of the Lord, openly contradicting here what the Lord has taught us to pray for? If God does not lead us into temptation, why should we then ask him: "Lead us not into temptation"?

To explain this—perhaps only apparent—contradiction, we must first inquire as to the exact linguistic meaning of the petition. Since Jesus' original words in Aramaic and/or Hebrew have not been preserved for us, we can only attempt a reconstruction. Did Jesus mean that God himself "leads" us into the situation of being tempted? James is quite emphatically of a different opinion: "Each person is tempted when he is lured and enticed by his own desire" (Jas 1:14). The great Qumran scholar Jean Carmignac demonstrated in a meticulous study that the original meaning of this petition could be rendered more or less as follows: "Father, . . . see that we do not enter into temptation", or: "that we do not give in to temptation". And he refers to Jesus' most characteristic prayer to his Father and ours, which he uttered in the Cenacle: "I do not pray that you should take them out of the world, but that you should keep them from the evil one" (Jn 17:15).

From what temptation, though, might the Father keep

us? First of all, from the threat that lies within us: "Lord, save me from myself!", Saint Augustine prayed. It is a humble cry for help, which acknowledges how defenseless we are on our own against the things that can arise from the labyrinthine ways of our heart, from the mistakes and omissions of our past, or from sudden waves of passion and distress and become temptations for us. "Keep us from danger!"

Of all temptations, probably the worst is that we begin to have doubts about Jesus, about faith in him, about his so often hidden presence, about the nearness of his kingdom: "Blessed is he who takes no offense at me" (Lk 7:23). How well our Lord knows this threat to our fidelity to him, to the discipleship of taking up the cross and following him: "Simon, Simon, behold, Satan demanded to have you [that is, the disciples], that he might sift you [all] like wheat; but I have prayed for you [that is, Peter specifically] that your faith may not fail" (Lk 22:31–32). Yet we, too, should pray "that you may not enter into temptation" (Lk 22:40). How good it is to know that "we have an advocate with the Father, Jesus Christ the righteous" (1 Jn 2:1). Therefore fear should not predominate in this petition; after all, we trust in the One whom we, with Jesus, are allowed to call "Abba, Father" (Mk 14:36).

47

. . . But deliver us from evil

In the seventh petition of the Our Father we say, "deliver us from evil." What "evil" is supposed to mean was spelled out in the prayer that followed immediately afterward in the traditional Mass: "Deliver us, we beseech you, O Lord, from all evils, past, present, and to come." The new version of this prayer after the [postconciliar] liturgical reform has been incorporated into the final petition: "Deliver us from evil. . . ."

From evil, from the evil one: Which sort of liberation and deliverance should we pray for? The Greek word can "be understood personally and objectively and thus can mean either *the evil one* or *evil*" (H. Schürmann). In order to do justice to both of these possibilities, the new German ecumenical translation of the prayer has settled on "*von dem Bösen*" [from the evil one]. The primary meaning of the petition is probably the personal one: it "refers to a person, Satan, the Evil One, the angel who opposes God" (CCC 2851). Together with him, however, is meant all the evil that oppresses and threatens us. Implied also is the long litany of ills caused by the workings of the evil one, both physical and spiritual, those that have already happened and those that are still impending. "From famine, pestilence, and war, O Lord, deliver us", reads an ancient prayer of supplication, arising from a multifarious experience of distress.

All human needs can be included in this petition

(CCC 2854). People came to Jesus with all sorts of needs; he turned no one away, even if he did not free all of them from all their ills. This is because many of them are supposed to be endured, perhaps even taken up willingly as a cross. Many a difficulty proves to be a grace-filled way.

If Jesus teaches us to pray to the Father for deliverance from the evil one, then this should also teach us to discern which evil we really ought to fear: "Do not fear those who kill the body but cannot kill the soul; rather fear him who can destroy both soul and body in hell" (Mt 10:28).

Therefore we should pray, not only that the Father will not allow us to run into temptation, but also that he will even "snatch us back" when the evil one menacingly draws near: "We feel so weak and endangered that we do not even want to live in his 'vicinity'" (H. Schürmann).

Two more notes: "Deliver us . . ."—together, not every man for himself; rather, all pray for one another, because we all need this deliverance.

And: evil there will always be, as long as we are on earth, as long as evil dwells in human hearts and the evil one is active. That is why this petition looks to a final, definitive deliverance from evil, to the fulfillment of "our blessed hope", the glorious coming of our "Savior Jesus Christ" (Tit 2:13).

48

Prayer to Jesus

Jesus taught us, with complete confidence, to turn in prayer to God as our Father. Yet there is no doubt that from the earliest times prayer has also been directed to Jesus himself: "Son of David, have mercy on me!" (Mk 10:48), cries the blind man from Jericho, Bartimaeus. And many others plead with him in a similar way (CCC 2616). Can such requests be understood as prayer in the strict sense of the word? Is it not simply asking someone whom many believe to be capable of helping and healing? Prayer in the proper sense can refer only to God. We cannot "adore" or pray to even the mightiest human helper, however much we may reverence and love him.

May Jesus, the Christ, the Son of God (cf. Mt 16:16), be adored and glorified in the same way as the Father? What place should Christ have in prayer? Most of the prayers that we recite in the Mass, especially during the Eucharistic Prayer, are addressed to God the Father, of course "through our Lord Jesus Christ."

"Through him and with him and in him", we give the Father "all glory and honor". The Apostle Paul already prays in this way: "I thank my God through Jesus Christ for all of you" (Rom 1:8). Jesus is our great and unique Mediator and true Intercessor with the Father; he is our High Priest: "Consequently he is able for all time to save those who draw near to God through him, since he always lives to make intercession for them" (Heb 7:25).

The early Christian writer Tertullian describes Christianity concisely: "We worship God through Christ" (*Apologeticus* 21, 28). That is why the ancient Church and usually our liturgy today conclude prayer "by praising the Father through Christ Jesus in the Holy Spirit". Many concluded from this—following Arius—that the Son was less than the Father, a creature and not God. In order to ward off this misinterpretation, Saint Basil the Great began in the fourth century to pray: "To the Father be glory with the Son, together with the Holy Spirit."

A great controversy ensued, but the holy Church Father pointed to the word of Jesus himself, who had given to his disciples the instruction: "Make disciples of all nations, baptizing them in the name of the Father and of the Son and of the Holy Spirit" (Mt 28:19). And so we say to this day, when we make the sign of the cross. This is at the same time, though, the expression of our faith that Jesus is true God and true man and that we therefore do not only ask him in all our needs but can truly worship him as well. "We adore you, O Christ, and we bless you, because by your holy Cross you have redeemed the world." That is also why the shortest and most fervent prayer is to pronounce, lovingly and adoringly, the name "which is above every name" (Phil 2:9): "Jesus!"

49

Come, Creator Spirit!

Jesus has taught us to pray to God as our Father. The
confidence to pray in this way, however, is granted
by the Spirit, whom Jesus promised to his disciples and
who was poured out upon them on Pentecost. "We
have received the Spirit, who makes us children of God.
Therefore, full of confidence, we pray: Our Father . . .":
thus one introduction to the Lord's Prayer. Yet how
often do we not know "how to pray as we ought, but
the Spirit himself intercedes for us with sighs too deep
for words" (Rom 8:26).

Who is he, this Counselor whom Jesus promised and
sent from the Father (cf. Jn 14:16, 15:26, 16:13)? If he
comes to help us in our weakness (cf. Rom 8:26), then
we can also ask him for help: "Come!" But then he is
not some "thing", an anonymous power, but rather some
One, the Holy Spirit.

Because the Church, from her earliest days, waits in
prayer at Jesus' command for the coming of the Spirit
(cf. Acts 1:8–14), she becomes more and more aware
that she, too, can pray directly to the Holy Spirit, that he
is God, worshipped and glorified with the Father and
the Son.

The simplest prayer to the Holy Spirit is the petition,
"Come!" (CCC 2671). It springs from a yearning for the
"indwelling" of God in us through the Holy Spirit (cf.
Rom 5:5). It is nourished by a living faith in the pres-

ence of the Holy Spirit, who dwells within us, since in Baptism we have become his temple.

One of the great spiritual masters of our days, Father Marie-Eugène Grialou, O.C.D., says on this subject: "I would like to encourage you to believe in the Holy Spirit, who dwells in your soul. God's Spirit is not an idea or a reality hovering in the clouds. He is Someone! He dwells in us; he is the life of the soul; he is its living Breath, its abiding Guest; he works unceasingly in us. He is a living, intelligent, loving Person within us. Let us make a resolution, therefore, to live with this Spirit, to call on him now and then, indeed, to visit him often." [1]

The Holy Spirit is the soul of prayer, just as he is, so to speak, the soul of the Church (CCC 797). He is the interior fountain from which streams of light and life flow. "He is there, our Friend; he is there, our Guest; he is there, the Architect of the Church; he is there, the Worker of our sanctification! He is there, the Master Builder of the Church, of this great work into which he incorporates us." [2]

Intimacy with the Holy Spirit is therefore also the soul of any fruitful apostolate. This consists of "cooperation with the working of the Holy Spirit".[3]

All the more urgent, then, is our prayer: "Come!"

---

[1] *In der Kraft des Geistes, Gebet und Apostolat* [In the power of the Spirit: Prayer and apostolate] (Leutesdorf, 1997), p. 193.

[2] Ibid.

[3] Ibid., p. 194.

50

Pray with Mary; to her, also?

"You shall worship the Lord your God and him only shall you serve"; so Jesus answers the tempter, who challenges him in the desert to worship him (Mt 4:10). We worship God, the Father, the Son, and the Holy Spirit—him, the triune God alone. We may not worship any creature, not even the holiest, not even Mary. May we pray to her, though? "Mary, to thee do we cry", we sing in beloved Marian invocations. In the countless Marian sanctuaries of the world, prayers are offered unceasingly: to God, of course, but also to Mary. Is she not being mistaken for God after all, "idolized," as the accusation of many Protestant Christians maintains?

Their concern may be justified in cases where Mary's "messages" become more important than God's Word, where the out-of-the-ordinary is sought more than the sober faith on account of which Elizabeth called Mary blessed (Lk 1:45). But where Mary herself is loved and honored in faith, she is also the surest way to Christ.

"Do whatever he tells you" (Jn 2:5)—this is one of the few things said by Mary that the Gospels have handed down. It is a challenge to imitate her, who entered with all her being into relation with God's Word and will: "I am the handmaid of the Lord; let it be to me according to your word" (Lk 1:38).

The basis for prayer to Mary is a simple, straightforward faith in what God has accomplished through and with Mary. Together with Mary, the Church from the earliest times has praised God, because he has done great things for her (cf. Lk 1:49): "Behold, henceforth all generations will call me blessed" (Lk 1:48). Grateful for her faith and her devotion to God's will, the Church salutes her. From this, naturally—how could it be otherwise?—developed a unique confidence that Mary has a heart for everyone for whom her Son laid down his life. With the sure instinct of faith that the Holy Spirit gives, the People of God sensed that Mary is especially close to the "favorites" of Jesus: the little ones, the poor, the sinners, the "brokenhearted" (cf. Ps 51:17).

Possibly from as early as the third century comes the prayer that is well known in its later form: "We fly to your patronage, O holy Mother of God. Despise not our prayers in our necessities, but ever deliver us from all dangers, O glorious and blessed Virgin" (cf. *Lumen Gentium*, no. 66). Mary is our "model of prayer" and "intercessor": "We can pray with and to her. The prayer of the Church is sustained by the prayer of Mary and united with it in hope" (CCC 2679).

51

Angels and prayer

"Are they not all ministering spirits sent forth to serve, for the sake of those who are to obtain salvation?" So the Letter to the Hebrews (1:14) speaks about the angels (CCC 331). The world of the Bible is acquainted with them; they are mysterious and yet very near, close to the mystery of God and close to men.

Many are of the opinion that they are quite far removed from "modern man". How is this view to be reconciled with the fact that currently books about angels are doing a "booming business"? Often forgotten in preaching and neglected in theology, they are nevertheless quite close to us men with their protective care. It is a rare hymn that stirs hearts as much as the poem written by Dietrich Bonhoeffer in prison in 1944 while facing death: "With kindly powers watching us and warning, / we wait in consolation, come what may. / God is with us at evening, in the morning, / and most assuredly with each new day."

Maybe we ought to reflect a moment and realize how often the angels are mentioned in our prayers. Right at the beginning of Holy Mass we say in the Penitential Rite: "And I ask blessed Mary, ever virgin, all the angels and saints, and you, my brothers and sisters, to pray for me to the Lord our God." Thus we commend ourselves to the intercessory prayer of the angels.

They are praying beings; they go before us in prayer,

and we join in their prayer; these things are expressed in every Preface of the Mass, when the celebrant prays, for example: "Therefore with the angels and archangels, the thrones and dominations and all the multitudes of the heavenly host, we sing the hymn of your glory: Holy, Holy, Holy. . . ." At the Gloria during Mass, too, we join our voices with the song of praise that the angels sang at the birth of Christ (Lk 2:14): "Glory to God in the highest, and on earth peace among men with whom he is pleased" (Lk 2:14). And again and again on solemn occasions we sing in the hymn "Holy God, We Praise Thy Name": "Hark, the loud celestial hymn / Angel choirs above are raising, / Cherubim and Seraphim, / in unceasing chorus praising, / fill the heavens with sweet accord: / Holy, Holy, Holy Lord!"

How is it, then, that we are not better acquainted with them, these magnificent creatures who are so near to God and to us? The answer of the Bible is clear: The angels are especially near to people who pray. Those invisible beings, who live in constant contemplation of God, will always come to the help of those who seek interior converse with God. This is especially true of children (cf. Mt 18:10). And of Mary, to whom the Angel Gabriel brought the good news (Lk 1:26). So we, too, can be confident and ask the angels to bring our prayer "before the face of God" and to "lend wings" to us as we pray.

O my God, Trinity

Usually we begin our prayers with the sign of the cross, "in the name of the Father and of the Son and of the Holy Spirit". The ways in which we believe, celebrate, live, and pray have their origin and their goal in the mystery of God. The *Catechism* begins with God, when it says: "God, infinitely perfect and blessed in himself, in a plan of sheer goodness freely created man to make him share in his own blessed life" (CCC 1).

That is our goal: to be admitted into the everlasting happiness of the triune God. All of God's works serve this purpose: creation and redemption, God's providence and the workings of his grace. Yet this goal is not found exclusively at an unattainable distance at the end of the path. It is already here present. Even now we are destined to live in the communion of the Trinity. Even now we are united with Christ, as members of his Body; we have received the Holy Spirit, "who makes us children of God"; even now we can call God our Father, because we are not merely called children of God—that is what we really are (cf. 1 Jn 3:1). "Hence the whole Christian life is a communion with each of the divine persons, without in any way separating them. Everyone who glorifies the Father does so through the Son in the Holy Spirit; everyone who follows Christ does so because the Father draws him [cf. Jn 6:44] and the Spirit moves him [cf. Rom 8:14]" (CCC 259).

This is especially true of our prayer. Even when we pray to the Father as Jesus taught us, we do it thanks to the intimacy that Jesus has enabled us to have with the Father, and the Holy Spirit brings about this confidence in us (cf. Rom 8:15, Gal 4:6): "In the New Covenant, prayer is the living relationship of the children of God with their Father who is good beyond measure, with his Son Jesus Christ and with the Holy Spirit. The grace of the Kingdom is 'the union of the entire holy and royal Trinity . . . with the whole human spirit' [Saint Gregory of Nazianzus, *Oratio*, 16, 9: PG 35, 945]. Thus, the life of prayer is the habit of being in the presence of the thrice-holy God and in communion with him" (CCC 2565).

If we look into the prayer life of the saints, it offers testimony again and again to the joyful certainty: God the Trinity is already with us now, and even more: he dwells in us (cf. Jn 14:23); in our hearts he waits for us; we can meet him. With Blessed Elizabeth of the Trinity, we conclude these "Paths of Prayer": "O my God, Trinity whom I adore, help me forget myself entirely so as to establish myself in you, unmovable and peaceful as if my soul were already in eternity."

Abbreviations

CCC   *Catechism of the Catholic Church*, 2d ed., revised in accordance with the official Latin text (1997)

DV   Vatican II, Dogmatic Constitution on Divine Revelation, *Dei Verbum* (November 18, 1965)

PL   J. P. Migne, ed. *Patrologia Latina* (Paris, 1841–1855)

PG   J. P. Migne, ed. *Patrologia Graeca* (Paris, 1857–1866)